Reading *Religious Affections*

Other Titles by Solid Ground

In addition to Reading *Religious Affections* by Biehl, we are delighted to offer several titles connected with Old Princeton.

Notes on Galatians by Machen is a reprint that is long overdue, especially in light of the present-day battle of the doctrine articulated in Galatians.

The Origin of Paul's Religion by Machen penetrates to the heart of the matter and speaks to many of the contemporary attacks upon the purity of the Gospel of Christ.

Biblical and Theological Studies by the professors of Princeton in 1912, at the centenary celebration of the Seminary. Articles are by men like Allis, Vos, Warfield, Machen, Wilson and others.

Theology on Fire: Vols. 1 & 2 by J.A. Alexander is the two volumes of sermons by this brilliant scholar from Princeton Seminary.

A Shepherd's Heart by J.W. Alexander is a volume of outstanding expository sermons from the pastoral ministry of one of the leading preachers of the 19th century.

Evangelical Truth by Archibald Alexander is a volume of practical sermons intended to be used for Family Worship.

The Lord of Glory by B.B. Warfield is one of the best treatments of the doctrine of the Deity of Christ ever written. Warfield is simply masterful.

The Power of God unto Salvation by B.B. Warfield is the first book of sermons ever published of this master-theologian. Several of these are found nowhere else.

The Person & Work of the Holy Spirit by B.B. Warfield is a compilation of all the sermons, articles and book reviews by a master-theologian on a theme that should interest every child of God. Brilliant in every way!

Grace & Glory by Geerhardus Vos is a series of addresses delivered in the chapel to the students at Princeton. John Murray said of him, "Dr. Vos is, in my judgment, the most penetrating exegete it has been my privilege to know, and I believe, the most incisive exegete that has appeared in the English-speaking world in this century."

Princeton Sermons: *Chapel Addresses from 1891-92* by B.B. Warfield, W.H. Green, C.W. Hodge, John D. Davis and More. According to Joel Beeke, this is "a treasure-trove of practical Christianity delivered by some of the greatest preachers and seminary teachers America has ever known."

Call us at **1-205-443-0311**
Send us an e-mail at **mike.sgcb@gmail.com**
Visit us on line at **www.solid-ground-books.com**

Reading *Religious Affections*

A Study Guide to Jonathan Edwards' Classic on the Nature of True Christianity

Craig Biehl

SOLID GROUND CHRISTIAN BOOKS
BIRMINGHAM, ALABAMA USA

Solid Ground Christian Books
PO Box 660132
Vestavia Hills AL 35266
205-443-0311
mike.sgcb@gmail.com
www.solid-ground-books.com

READING *RELIGOUS AFFECTIONS*
*A Study Guide to Jonathan Edwards' Classic
on the Nature of True Christianity*

by Craig Biehl

© Craig Biehl, 2012, All Rights Reserved.

First Solid Ground edition in April 2012

Cover design by Borgo Design
Contact them at borgogirl@bellsouth.net

ISBN- 978-159925-277-3

Table of Contents

Analytical Outline iii

Foreword iv

Author's Preface v

Part One: Background, Nature, and Importance of Religious Affections 1

    Session One: Introduction to Jonathan and Sarah Edwards 2

    Session Two: The Context and Occasion of *The Religious Affections*: The Great Awakening 7

    Session Three: Definition, Nature, Importance, and Scripture Support of Religious Affections 17

Part Two: Uncertain Signs that Religious Affections are the Work of God in a True Believer ... 27

    Session Four 28

        Introduction 28

        Sign I: Religious Fervor or Zeal 29

        Sign II: Great Physical Affects on the Body 30

        Sign III: Fluent, Fervent, and Abundant Religious Talk 31

    Session Five 33

        Sign IV: That Affections Seem To Be from an External Supernatural Source 33

        Sign V: That Religious Affections Come with Texts of Scripture in the Mind 35

        Sign VI: The Presence of Love 35

        Sign VII: The Presence of Many Kinds of Religious Affections Accompanying Each Other 35

    Session Six 39

        Sign VIII: That Joy and Comfort Follow Conviction and Mourning for Sin 39

        Sign IX: Great Time and Energy Spent in Religious Activity and Worship 42

        Sign X: Abundant Praise to God 43

    Session Seven 45

        Sign XI: Great Assurance of One's Own Salvation 45

    Session Eight 54

        Sign XII: That One's Religious Affections and Testimonies Move the Hearts of Saints 54

Part Three: True Signs of God's Work in the Affections of a True Believer 58

    Session Nine: Qualifications and the Fruit of the Permanent Indwelling of the Holy Spirit 59

        Introduction and Necessary Qualifications 59

Sign I: Gracious Affections (Religious Affections that Are a Work of God in a True Believer) Are the Fruit of the Holy Spirit that Dwells Permanently in the Believer........ 60

Session Ten 70

Sign II: Gracious Affections Are Founded Primarily upon the Greatness of God and His Works, Apart from Self-Interest 70

Session Eleven 77

Sign III: Gracious Affections Are Founded upon the "Loveliness" of the Holiness of God and His Works 77

Session Twelve 84

Sign IV: Gracious Affections Arise from Divine Illumination 84

Session Thirteen 91

Sign V: Gracious Affections Are Accompanied by the Conviction that the Gospel Is True 91

Session Fourteen 97

Sign VI: Gracious Affections Are Accompanied by True Humility 97

Session Fifteen 104

Sign VII: Gracious Affections Accompany a Change of Nature 104

Sign VIII: Gracious Affections Promote and Are Attended with a Christ-Like Demeanor 105

Session Sixteen 110

Sign IX: Gracious Affections "Soften the Heart" 110

Sign X: Gracious Affections Have a Beautiful Symmetry and Balance 111

Sign XI: The Higher Gracious Affections Are Raised, the Greater the Desire for Spiritual Growth, Whereas False Affections Rest Satisfied in Themselves 115

Session Seventeen 118

Sign XII: Gracious Affections Generate Christian Practice and Fruit (Part 1) 118

Session Eighteen 126

Sign XII: Gracious Affections Generate Christian Practice and Fruit (Part 2) 126

Session Nineteen 131

Sign XII: Gracious Affections Generate Christian Practice and Fruit (Part 3) 131

Session Twenty 135

Sign XII: Gracious Affections Generate Christian Practice and Fruit (Part 4) 135

Analytical Outline

Part One: Background, Nature, and Importance of Religious Affections

1. Introduction to Jonathan and Sarah Edwards.
2. The Context and Occasion of the Writing of *The Religious Affections*: The Glories, Evils, and Confusion of the Great Awakening
3. The Essence of True Christianity
4. The Nature and Definition of Religious Affections
5. Scriptural Evidence of the Centrality and Importance of Religious Affections to the Christian Life
6. Implications for Proper Theology and Christian Living

Part Two: Uncertain Signs that Religious Affections are the Work of God in a True Believer

1. Religious Fervor and Zeal
2. Great Physical Effects on the Body (fainting, groaning, shaking, etc.)
3. Fluent, Fervent, and Abundant Religious Talk
4. That Affections Seem To Be From an External Supernatural Source
5. That Religious Affections Come with Texts of Scripture in the Mind
6. The Presence of Love
7. The Presence of Many Kinds of Religious Affections Accompanying Each Other
8. That Joy and Comfort Follow Conviction and Mourning for Sin
9. Great Time and Energy Spent in Religious Activity and Worship
10. Abundant Praise to God
11. Great Assurance of One's Salvation
12. That One's Religious Affections and Testimonies Move the Hearts of Saints

Part Three: True Signs of God's Work in the Affections of a True Believer ("Gracious Affections")

1. Gracious Affections Are the Fruit of the Holy Spirit Dwelling Permanently in the Believer
2. Gracious Affections Are Founded Primarily upon the Greatness of God and His Works, Apart from Self-Interest
3. Gracious Affections are Founded upon the "Loveliness" of the Holiness of God
4. Gracious Affections Arise from Divine Illumination, Not Natural Reason
5. Gracious Affections are Accompanied by the Conviction that the Gospel Is True
6. Gracious Affections are Accompanied by True Biblical Humility
7. Gracious Affections Accompany a Change of Nature
8. Gracious Affections Promote a Christ-like Demeanor
9. Gracious Affections Soften the Heart
10. Gracious Affections Have a Beautiful Symmetry and Balance
11. Gracious Affections are Not Self-Satisfied, but, Desire to Love God More
12. Gracious Affections Result in Christian Practice and Perseverance

Foreword

Religious Affections. The phrase has almost become synonymous with Jonathan Edwards and the Great Awakening of the eighteenth century. Edwards used the term in his famous *Treatise Concerning Religious Affections* of 1746, and many revivalists and theologians after him have used it to identify the experience of enlightened recipients of God's grace. Today we say that someone is "affectionate" when they are loving or caring. And while Edwards held that love is the defining quality of religion, manifest in motive and behavior, religious affections entail more than love or being affectionate.

In the Christian tradition, some claim that knowledge of God comes through human reason, while others believe it comes through human emotions. But affections cannot be reduced to the "heart" versus the "head." All too often and too easily readers and interpreters of Edwards tend to equate affections with "feelings" or "passions." But that is too simplistic. For Edwards, affections are acts of the will informed by understanding, involving both heart *and* head. Even more, he saw that affections have *degrees*. And the extent to which we have affections can be a key to knowing whether our tendencies lie towards self or towards God. Gracious affections are therefore *holy*, that is, they have the beauty of God's excellence as their object.

In this study guide to Edwards' *Religious Affections*, Craig Biehl leads teachers and students through the categories of religious experience that Edwards identifies in order to help individuals discern between true and false Christianity, and to examine their own experiences for "signs" or "marks" of counterfeit and true grace. Edwards did this not with any pretense that his signs or marks were infallible—only God is the true searcher of hearts—but rather to help believers to re-examine their assumptions about their religious state, and spur them on to a deeper love of God and true holiness. Through excerpts from Edwards, secondary interpretive readings, contemporary sources, Scripture texts, and study questions, the reader is provided with a step-by-step method for a thoughtful and reflective approach to the ultimate Christian question: Am I a true Christian? As Jesus said, the way is "strait," meaning narrow and difficult. But the work is worth the effort. May this resource be a blessing to those seeking to ascertain the nature of their own religious affections.

Dr. Kenneth P. Minkema
Jonathan Edwards Center, Yale University

Author's Preface

Contemporary readers unfamiliar with Edwards' 18th Century English have found *Religious Affections* an arduous read. Yet, the greater difficulty reading Edwards, I believe, is following the comprehensive and exacting nature of his arguments. Edwards' definitions and explanations are meticulous and exhaustive, his sentences are long and weighty, while the logic of a single point can carry on for pages. Few contemporary readers are trained to think as carefully as 18th Century theologians, let alone one as profound as Edwards. His arguments are carefully and brilliantly crafted, but they require time and effort to grasp.

The following summary and outline of Edwards' monumental classic was developed for application to a teaching setting to help address this particular need. The logic, flow, and structure of Edwards' arguments are more easily seen in the format of a detailed outline. So designed, the study guide is intended to supplement, not replace, the reading of *Religious Affections*. Edwards chose his words carefully, so any summary or abridgment of his words will necessarily diminish the brilliance of his argumentation. Thus, my hope is that this study guide will provide an additional aid to encourage the direct study of *Religious Affections* in churches, colleges and seminaries.[1]

The study guide is divided into twenty teaching modules, with discussion questions following each module. As Edwards' theological insights are as applicable today as they were at the time of its initial publication in 1746, the discussion questions are designed to help teachers and students apply them to their own heart and to contemporary Christianity in general. Scripture references are sometimes written out to expedite the pace of the study, while references listed without text allow teachers and students to look up verses to interact with their own Bibles as part of the study.

Quotations in the study guide are taken from the Banner of Truth version of *Religious Affections*, but are all cross referenced to the Yale edition. Thus, the study guide can be used with both the Banner of Truth or Yale versions.

Many thanks to Ken Minkema of the Jonathan Edwards Center of Yale University for his kind assistance, editorial critiques, and encouragement to publish the study guide. I am grateful to the elders at Believer's Chapel in Dallas, Texas, where I first developed and taught through the study guide in 1994. And thanks to Andrew and Teresa Schaeckenbach for their support and delightful hospitality during that time. Most importantly, all thanks and praise to the excellent God and Savior of Edwards, the source of all true and holy religious affections.

---

[1] For an additional aid to reading *Religious Affections*, see C. Samuel Storms, *Signs of the Spirit: An Interpretation of Jonathan Edwards's "Religious Affections"* (Wheaton: Crossway Books, 2007).

PART ONE

Background, Nature, and Importance of Religious Affections

SESSION ONE

Introduction to Jonathan and Sarah Edwards

Suggested Reading:

- George Marsden, *Jonathan Edwards: A Life*. Yale University Press, 2003.
- Iain Murray, *Jonathan Edwards: A New Biography*. The Banner of Truth Trust, 1987.
- Edna Gerstner, *Jonathan and Sarah: An Uncommon Union*. Soli Deo Gloria, 1995.

I. Introduction to Jonathan Edwards (1703-1758)

    A) His reputation

        1) Positively

"The profoundest reasoner, and the greatest divine, in my opinion, that America ever produced."[2]

"He was, in the estimation of the writer, one of the most holy, humble and heavenly minded men, that the world has seen, since the apostolic age."[3]

"The Greatest, wisest, humblest and holiest of uninspired men."[4]

"Never was there a happier combination of great power with great piety."[5]

"Edwards was extraordinary. By many estimates, he was the most acute early American philosopher and the most brilliant of all American theologians. At least three of his many works—*Religious Affections, Freedom of the Will,* and *The Nature of True Virtue*—stand as masterpieces in the larger history of Christian literature."[6]

"No man is more relevant to the present condition of Christianity than Jonathan Edwards….He was a mighty theologian and a great evangelist at the same time….He was pre-eminently the theologian of revival. If you want to know anything about true revival, Edwards is the man to consult."[7]

---

[2] Samuel Davies, 1759; quoted in Iain Murray, *Jonathan Edwards: A New Biography* (Banner of Truth Trust: Edinburgh, 1987; reprint, 1988), xv.
[3] Ashbel Green, President of the College of New Jersey, 1822; quoted in Murray, *Jonathan Edwards*, xv.
[4] A note in John Collett Ryland's copy of Hopkins' Life of Edwards; quoted in Murray, *Jonathan Edwards*, xv.
[5] Thomas Chalmers, quoted by G. D. Henderson in 'Jonathan Edwards and Scotland', *The Evangelical Quarterly*, January 1944; quoted in Murray, *Jonathan Edwards*, xvi.
[6] George M. Marsden, *Jonathan Edwards: A Life* (Yale University Press: New Haven, 2003) 1.
[7] D. Martyn Lloyd-Jones, 1976; quoted in Murray, *Jonathan Edwards*, xvii.

2) Negatively

"A visionary enthusiast, and not to be minded in anything he says."[8]

"The life of Edwards is a tragedy....Because of his faith Edwards wrought incalculable harm....a more repulsive individual never influenced history."[9]

"If he had lived a hundred years later and breathed the air of freedom, he could not have written with such old-world barbarism as we find in his volcanic sermons."[10]

"His philosophical insight was buried under the ruins of his religion. He failed to see the futility of insisting on the Puritan principles."[11]

3) What accounts for the difference of opinion regarding Edwards?

"Here is the fundamental reason why opinions on Edwards are so divided, and why his biographers should also differ so widely. The division runs right back to the Bible, and, depending on where we stand in relation to Christ, we shall join ourselves to one side or the other in interpreting this man who was, first of all, a Christian."[12]

B) Personal highlights

- 1703: Born to Timothy and Esther (Stoddard) Edwards
- Proficient in Latin, Greek, and Hebrew by age 13
- 1720: BA, Yale
- 1722: MA, Yale
- 1729: Elected Pastor of Congregational Church in Northampton, Massachusetts
- 1746: *The Religious Affections* published
- 1750: Dismissed from Northampton church over disagreement regarding who may participate in the Lord's Table, among other things. Moved to Stockbridge to minister to the Indians.
- 1757: Elected president of Princeton
- 1758: Died from Smallpox vaccination

---

[8] Charles Chauncy, quoted in Murray, *Jonathan Edwards*, xxiii.
[9] Perry Miller, *Jonathan Edwards* (The University of Massachusetts Press: Amherst, 1949), 16, 148, 153; quoted in Murray, *Jonathan Edwards*, xxi, xxiii.
[10] Oliver Wendell Holmes, quoted in Murray, *Jonathan Edwards*, xx.
[11] Herbert Schneider, quoted in Murray, *Jonathan Edwards*, xxi.
[12] Murray, *Jonathan Edwards*, xxvi-xxvii. Modern scholarship on Edwards exhibits a similar tendency. Beginning with Perry Miller, Edwards scholars have often secularized Edwards in downplaying or ignoring his Christ-centered theology or in treating his philosophical writings in abstraction from his biblical foundation and focus. Edwards is thereby made more acceptable to modern scholarship. In addition, many scholars have made Edwards into their own image by reading their own theology and worldview into his writings. One must read Edwards to truly understand Edwards, as the secondary literature can be misleading. For a brief summary of the history of Edwards scholarship, see the Introduction in Craig Biehl, *The Infinite Merit of Christ: The Glory of Christ's Obedience in the Theology of Jonathan Edwards* (Jackson, MS: Reformed Academic Press, 2009).

Timothy Edwards, Jonathan's father, was a faithful minster with earned B.A. and M.A. degrees from Harvard. He was "an effective preacher of revival" and "an expert on the science of conversion."[13] Jonathan was acquainted with "awakenings" from a young age. "According to Jonathan's later estimation, of all the pastors in the region, only his grandfather, Solomon Stoddard, oversaw more local awakenings" than his father Timothy Edwards.[14]

Jonathan had ten sisters and was the only son in a family of eleven siblings.

C) His view of the family

"We have had great disputes how the church ought to be regulated; and indeed the subject of these disputes was of great importance: but the due regulation of your families is of no less, and in some respects, of much greater importance. Every Christian family ought to be as it were a little church, consecrated to Christ, and wholly influenced and governed by his rules. And family education and order are some of the chief of the means of grace. If these fail, all other means are like to prove ineffectual. If these are duly maintained, all the means of grace will be like to prosper and be successful."[15]

D) His preaching

"A preacher of low and moderate voice, a natural way of delivery, and without any agitation of body, or anything else in the manner to excite attention, except his habitual and great solemnity, looking and speaking as in the presence of God."[16]

"What is clear is that the impression made by Edwards as a preacher owed little to the actual manner of his delivery. His voice was low and calm. He aimed to avoid 'a sad tone' and the 'very ridiculous whining tone' which he heard from some men. 'He made but little motion with his head or hands,' observes Hopkins. What was striking was the distinctness and clarity of his thought ('he handled concepts,' in McGiffert's phrase, 'as scrupulously and precisely as a banker handles currency') together with a seriousness arising from 'a solemn consciousness of the presence of God'. This seriousness, says Dwight, 'was visible in his looks and general demeanor. It obviously had a controlling influence over all his preparations for the pulpit.' On the same point he quotes Hopkins: 'He appeared with such gravity and solemnity, and his words were so full of ideas, that few speakers have been able to command the attention of an audience as he did.'"[17]

---

[13] Marsden, *Jonathan Edwards*, 25, 26.
[14] Marsden, *Jonathan Edwards*, 25.
[15] Jonathan Edwards, "A Farewell Sermon Preached at the First Precinct in Northampton, After the People's Public Rejection of their Minister…on June 22, 1750," in *Sermons and Discourses 1743-1758*, ed. Wilson H. Kimnach, *The Works of Jonathan Edwards*, vol. 25 (New Haven: Yale University Press, 2006), 484.
[16] John Gillies, quoted in Murray, *Jonathan Edwards*, 175.
[17] Murray, *Jonathan Edwards*, 191.

II. Introduction to Sarah Edwards and the Edwards Household

"Felt great satisfaction in being at the house of Mr. Edwards. A sweeter couple I have not yet seen. Their children were not dressed in silks and satins, but plain, as become the children of those who, in all things, ought to be examples of Christian simplicity. Mrs. Edwards is adorned with a meek and quiet spirit; she talked solidly of the things of God, and seemed to be such a helpmeet for her husband, that she caused me to renew those prayers, which, for some months, I have put up to God, that he would be pleased to send me a daughter of Abraham to be my wife."[18]

"Very courteously treated here. The most agreeable family I was ever acquainted with. Much of the presence of God here."[19]

"Edwards preached against husbands who 'treated their wives like servants' and who failed to 'study to suit' their partner. No one could suppose that Sarah's heavy share of labour in directing the home was due to any thoughtlessness on his part. Their respective work was happily agreed. 'No person of discernment could be conversant in the family,' writes Hopkins, 'without observing and admiring the great harmony and mutual love and esteem that subsisted between them.'"[20]

Sarah Edwards had a "lasting impact" on Samuel Hopkins, "Edwards' best known successor" and first biographer. "His biographical memoir, published in 1765, included a glowing tribute to Sarah. Admiring her for, among other virtues, having 'the law of kindness on her tongue,' Hopkins' portrait follows that same rule. He described her as 'a more than ordinary beautiful person; of a pleasant, agreeable countenance.' The genuineness of her piety was manifested in her concerns for charity toward the poor and her extraordinary kindness to guests and strangers. Moreover, she 'paid proper deference to Mr. Edwards,' catered to the peculiarities of his Spartan diet, and was a tender nurse to him in his illness. She too frequently 'labored under bodily disorders and pains' but cheerfully and without complaint."[21]

Questions and Points for Discussion

1) Iain Murray notes that the disparate opinions of Edwards can be traced to different opinions concerning the God of Edwards. What does this tell you about the ministry of Edwards, and what a faithful minister of Christ should expect in the court of public opinion?

---

[18] George Whitefield after a stay in the Edwards home, quoted in Murray, *Jonathan Edwards*, 178.
[19] Minister Joseph Emerson after a stay in the Edwards home, quoted in Murray, *Jonathan Edwards*, 185.
[20] Murray, *Jonathan Edwards*, 191-192. Samuel Hopkins was well-acquainted with the Edwards household, having lived in their home while studying with Mr. Edwards for upwards to a year from December of 1741 through 1742. See Stephen West, *Sketches of the Life of the Late, Rev. Samuel Hopkins, D. D.* (Hartford, 1805), 40-45.
[21] Marsden, *Jonathan Edwards*, 251.

2) Would the content and style of Edwards' preaching be popular today? Why or why not?

3) How and to what extent do you think Sarah Edwards' ministry as a homemaker was a factor in the depth and breadth of God's ministry through Jonathan Edwards?

4) Is Edwards' view of the family as one of God's "chief means of grace" applicable today? Would the application of his view of the family in contemporary Christian families prove beneficial to the church?

5) The greatest American theologian was dismissed from his church by a vote of his congregation. What lessons can be learned from this?

SESSION TWO

The Context and Occasion of **The Religious Affections**: *The Great Awakening*

Suggested Reading:

- Jonathan Edwards, *The Religious Affections*. Banner of Truth Trust, 1986, 9-20. Or, Jonathan Edwards, *The Religious Affections*. Yale University Press, 1959, 84-89.
- Edwin Scott Gaustad, The *Great Awakening in New England*. Harper & Brothers, 1957, 16-101.
- George Marsden, *Jonathan Edwards: A Life*. Yale University Press, 2003, 113-267.
- Iain Murray, *Jonathan Edwards: A New Biography*. Banner of Truth Trust, 1987, 153-248.
- Joseph Tracy, *The Great Awakening*. The Banner of Truth Trust, 1976, 230-255.

I. The State of the Churches in New England Prior to the Great Awakening

"By the time the eighteenth century was under way, New England had become a 'mixed multitude' religiously. The dominant religious group, Congregationalism, was losing its monopoly and its integrity as was the dominant theology, Calvinism. As sainthood became more synonymous with respectability, Congregationalism became more like the world in which it lived, less like a pure fellowship of saints called out from society....With the altered economy and the threat of rationalism, God became less respected as man became more respectable. It cannot both be that God and man are masters of all destiny. The decline of the Puritan piety was marked by a rise of 'many and great Impieties,' a fall in 'the power of godliness,' and a 'time of extraordinary dullness in religion.' New England, nodding sleepily, was soon to be awakened with a start."[22]

II. The Glories, Evils, and Confusion of the Great Awakening

"The Great Awakening of New England was not a series of isolated revival meetings, held over a period of several decades—as was the case in the middle and southern colonies. It was a rushing flood that swept over all the land, recognizing no boundaries, whether social, civil, or ecclesiastical, leaving no inhabited area untouched, and receding as suddenly as it had come."[23]

Though other awakenings in the colonies preceded and followed it, the Awakening from 1740-42 is often viewed as the *First* Great Awakening and is the Awakening primarily addressed by Edwards in *The Religious Affections*.

A) Positive and negative interpretations of the Awakening

1) Positively

---

[22] Edwin S. Gaustad, *The Great Awakening in New England* (Harper & Brothers: New York, 1957), 15
[23] Edwin S. Gaustad, "The Theological Effects of the Great Awakening in New England," *Mississippi Valley Historical Review* 40 (March 1954): 683; quoted in D. A. Sweeney, *Nathaniel Taylor, New Haven Theology, and the Legacy of Jonathan Edwards* (New York: Oxford University Press, 2003), 25.

"Religion is now much more the Subject of Conversation at Friends Houses, than ever I knew it. The Doctrines of Grace are espoused and relished. Private religions Meetings are greatly multiplied....There is indeed an extraordinary Appetite after the sincere Milk of the Word."[24]

"As people long'd more to hear; so Ministers lov'd more to preach than they used to do, and usually spoke with greater Power. Some of them that were Strangers to true and vital Piety before, became now acquainted with it; and others that were grown in a great Measure dead and formal, were quiken'd stir'd up, and had new life put into them. Some great and important Doctrines that before, if not wholly omitted, were but gently touch'd; were now more largely insisted on, more clearly unfolded, and more warmly press'd. Our Assemblies were vastly throng'd; and it was rare to see a careless and inattentive Hearer among them all. Their thirsty Souls seem'd greedily to drink down every Word that drop'd from the Preacher's lips."[25]

"Much more numerous and more frequently mentioned than the conversions were the signs of repentance and concern. William Cooper of Brattle Street Church remarked that in one week, at the height of the revival, more persons came to him in anxiety and concern than in the preceding twenty-four years of his ministry."[26]

2) Negatively

"Antinomian Principles are advanc'd, preach'd up and printed;--Christian Brethren have their Affections widely alienated;--Unchristian Censoriousness and hard judging abounds, Love stands afar of [sic], and Charity cannot enter;--Many Churches and Societies are broken and divided;--Pernicious and unjustifiable Separations are set up and continued....Numbers of illiterate Exhorters swarm about as Locusts from the Bottomless Pit:--We think upon the whole, that Religion is now in a far worse State than it was in 1740."[27]

"There never was such a Spirit of Superstition and Enthusiasm reigning in the Land before; never such gross Disorders and barefaced Affronts to common Decency; never such scandalous Reproaches on the Blessed Spirit, making him the Author of the greatest Irregularities and Confusions."[28]

"No greater mischief has arisen from any quarter. It is indeed the genuine force of infinite evil. Popery it self han't been the mother of more and greater blasphemies and abominations. It has made strong attempts to destroy all property, to make all things common, wives as well as goods.--It has promoted faction and contention; filled the church oftentimes with confusion, and the state sometimes with general disorder.--It has, by its pretended spiritual interpretations made void the most undoubted laws of God. It has laid aside the gospel sacraments as weak and carnal things; yea, this superior light within has, in the opinion of thousands, render'd the bible a useless dead letter.--It has made men fancy themselves to be prophets and apostles; yea, some have taken themselves to be Christ Jesus; yea, the blessed God

---

[24] William Cooper in *Distinguishing Marks*; quoted in Gaustad, *The Great Awakening*, 105.
[25] William Shurtleff; quoted in Gaustad, *The Great Awakening*, 102-3.
[26] Thomas Prince, *An Account*, 18; quoted in Gaustad, *The Great Awakening*, 104.
[27] Isaac Stiles, *The Declaration of the Association of the County of New-Haven in Connecticut* (1745); quoted in Gaustad, *The Great Awakening*, 103.
[28] Charles Chauncy in letter to Ezra Stiles; quoted in Gaustad, *The Great Awakening*, 88.

Background, Nature, and Importance of Religious Affections

himself. It has, in one word, been a pest to the church in all ages, as great an enemy to real and solid religion as perhaps the greatest infidelity."[29]

B) Problems and confusion within the Awakening

1) Error and excess

- Emotional excesses (fainting, screaming, shaking, etc.)
- Lack of order in worship services, including emotional excesses
- Zealous but contentious and theologically illiterate itinerant preachers
  - Lack of formal training
  - Presumptuous and destructive defamation of established ministers by itinerant preachers, often creating dissention and division within existing churches
- Claims of immediate revelation from God apart from Scripture
- Ostentatious displays of "boldness" and "spirituality"

Example: James Davenport (See Exhibits One to Three below)

2) Unbalanced ("all or nothing") responses to the positive and negative effects of the Awakening

Some pointed to the excesses and errors of the Awakening and wrongly concluded that none of the religious affections associated with the Awakening were from God. Others pointed to conversions and other positive aspects of the Awakening and wrongly concluded that all of the religious affections associated with the Awakening were from God.

Illustrated:

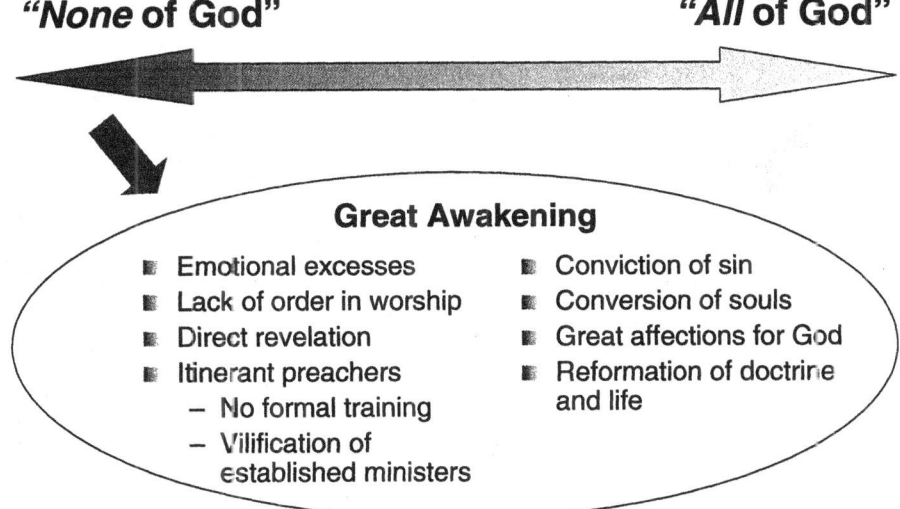

---

[29] Charles Chauncy, *Enthusiasm described and cautioned against... With a Letter to the Reverend Mr. James Davenport*, quoted in Gaustad, *The Great Awakening*, 87-88.

3) Theological illiteracy and error behind unbalanced interpretations of the Awakening

The various phenomena of the Awakening were interpreted differently according to different theological perspectives. There were exceptions, and theological perspectives and interpretations of the Awakening varied across a wide spectrum. But in general, the more rationalistic a religious perspective, and the more one discounted or rejected religious affections as essential to Christianity, the more likely the Awakening in its entirety was dismissed as not from God. The more experiential and mystical a religious perspective, and the more all religious affections were viewed as from God, the more likely the entirety of the Awakening was accepted as a work of God.

<u>Illustrated</u>:

"None of God"   "*All* of God"

- Reason as supreme
- Rationalism
- "Light"/No Heat
- ***Rejection of religious affections as essential to true religion***

- Experience as supreme
- Mysticism
- Heat/No Light
- ***Acceptance of all religious affections as evidence of true religion***

C) The "Old Light" vs. "New Light" schism

The debate as to whether or not the Great Awakening was from God split Congregationalism into two factions:[30]

1) <u>The Old Lights</u>: Those generally opposed to the Great Awakening

   Chief spokesman: Charles Chauncy (pastor of the First Church in Boston)

   Chauncy, though initially favorable toward the Awakening, eventually concluded from its attendant problems that it was godless and destructive in its entirety. In 1743, He wrote *Seasonal Thoughts on the State of Religion in New England* in response to Edwards' defense of the Awakening.

2) <u>The New Lights</u>: Those that viewed the Great Awakening as a great revival from God

   Chief spokesman: Jonathan Edwards

---

[30] A similar split occurred in the American colonies between "Old Side" Presbyterians (generally opposed the Awakening) and "New Side" Presbyterians (pro-Awakening).

Background, Nature, and Importance of Religious Affections   11

III. Edwards' Balanced Approach to the Great Awakening

A) Edwards sought an objective, theological appraisal of the Awakening.

Edwards, though a defender of the Awakening, actually stood in the middle between the two extreme positions. One the one hand, he opposed the view that accepted all the positive and negative aspects of the Awakening and uncritically affirmed all displays of religious affections as evidence of a true work of God. On the other hand, Edwards opposed the view that attributed all manifestations of religious affections during the Awakening to satanic delusion, depravity, weakness of disposition, or foolishness.

Illustrated:

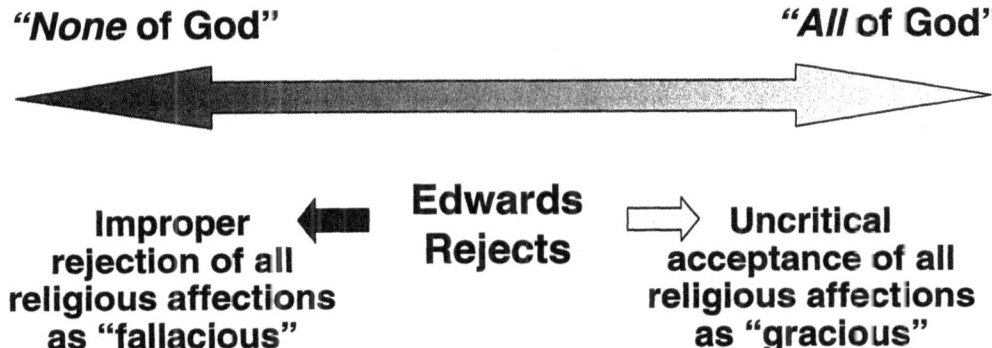

Edwards sought an objective appraisal of the Awakening that affirmed and supported that which was good and exposed and rejected that which was bad. He was not in favor of untrained ministers and he vigorously opposed the censoriousness, pride, and tendency of *some* itinerant preachers to pronounce the state of an individual's soul with certainty. Yet, he understood the importance of true affections to the Christian life. Edwards rejected the unbiblical and unbalanced principles behind the two extreme responses to the Awakening, while affirming the importance and necessity of religious affections as the fruit of the true saving work of the Holy Spirit in a believer.

Illustrated:

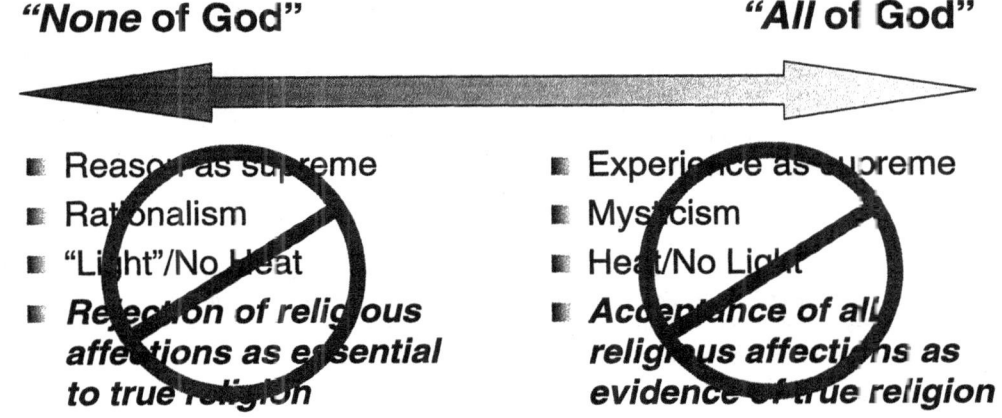

B) Edwards sought to identify and oppose the evils of the Awakening.

> "After religion has revived in the church of God, and enemies appear, people engaged to defend its cause are commonly most exposed where they are least sensible of danger. While they are wholly intent upon the opposition that appears openly before them, to make head against that, and do neglect carefully to look all around them, the devil comes behind them, and gives a fatal stab unseen; and has opportunity to give a more home stroke, and wound the deeper, because he strikes at his leisure and according to his pleasure, being obstructed by no guard or resistance."[31]

> "By this means he [Satan] brings it to pass, that men work wickedness under a notion of doing God service, and so sin without restraint, yea with earnest forwardness and zeal, and with all their might. By this means he brings in even the friends of religion, insensibly to themselves, to do the work of enemies, by destroying religion in a far more effectual manner than open enemies can do, under a notion of advancing it."[32]

IV. Edwards' Motives for Writing *The Religious Affections*

A) The need to discern and affirm good versus evil

> "It is by the mixture of counterfeit religion with true, not discerned and distinguished, that the devil has had his greatest advantage against the cause and kingdom of Christ all along."[33]

> "It is a hard thing to be a hearty zealous friend of what has been good and glorious in the late extraordinary appearances, and to rejoice much in it; and at the same time to see the evil and pernicious tendency of what has been bad, and earnestly to oppose that. But yet, I am humbly but firmly persuaded, we shall never be in the way of truth, nor go on in a way acceptable to God and tending to the advancement of Christ's kingdom, till we do so."[34]

B) The need for sound doctrinal understanding

> "In 1738 he [Edwards] published *Discourses on Various Important Subjects, Nearly Concerning the Great Affair of the Soul's Eternal Salvation*, a collection of sermons which he had preached during the peak of the religious excitement three to four years previously. Included here is Edwards' significant series on justification by faith, which doctrine, he now believes, was vindicated in and by the revival—'a remarkable Testimony of God's Approbation of the Doctrine.' Published because they were found to be particularly effective and plainly relevant, these discourses are notable for their lack of stirring emotional appeals. Filled with much theology and overflowing with ratiocination, they bowed the intellect before they swayed the heart. *Edwards regarded a doctrinal confusion rather than a lethargic disposition as the chief sore to be healed.*"[35]

---

[31] Jonathan Edwards, *The Religious Affections* (Edinburgh: Banner of Truth Trust, 1986), 18-19; hereafter cited as "BT." Cf. Jonathan Edwards, *Religious Affections*, ed. John Edwin Smith, *The Works of Jonathan Edwards*, vol. 2 (New Haven: Yale University Press, 1959), 87; hereafter cited as "Yale." All quotations in this study guide are taken from the Banner of Truth version, though the respective passage in the Yale volume will also be listed in each citation of BT.
[32] BT, 19; Yale, 88.
[33] BT, 17; Yale, 86.
[34] BT, 16; Yale, 85.
[35] Emphasis mine. Gaustad, *The Great Awakening*, 22.

Questions and Points for Discussion

1) An overreaction to error can create an equal or worse error. Can you identify contemporary or historical theological errors caused by an overreaction to error?

2) Is there a danger in theological discussion of adopting a party spirit and losing objectivity in analyzing a given issue scripturally? If so, how and why?

3) What does Scripture say concerning zeal without knowledge?

4) The professing church can be so occupied with the frontal attacks of the unbelieving world (rightfully so) that it neglects keeping its own house in order. The greatest hurt and shame to the church in the last century came at the hands of those naming the name of Christ. The professing church (not to assume all who *profess* Christ *possess* Christ) can sometimes be its own worst enemy. In what way do we face the same issues that faced Edwards in distinguishing the marks of true faith in Christ and the nature of true Christianity?

5) Just prior to the Great Awakening, the church in New England was lethargic and complacent, much like today. Yet, "Edwards regarded a doctrinal confusion rather than a lethargic disposition as the chief sore to be healed" and believed the intellect must be "bowed" before the heart can be "swayed." Is Edwards' diagnosis and prescription applicable for today? [You may want to revisit this question after completing the study guide, as your understanding may change as a result.]

6) God the Holy Spirit used the clear and uncompromised preaching of His written word (Scripture) to produce the greatest awakening in American history. Is there a lesson here for the church today?

Exhibit One: James Davenport's Excesses at New London in 1743

"By invitation of a company of his partisans, he arrived at New London, March 2, 1743, to organize them into a church. Immediately on his arrival, in obedience to messages which he said he had received from God in dreams and otherwise, he began to purify the company from evils which prevailed among them. To cure them of their idolatrous love of worldly things, he ordered wigs, cloaks, and breeches, hoods, gowns, rings, jewels and necklaces to be brought together into his room, and laid in a heap, that they might, by his solemn decree, be committed to the flames. To this heap he added the pair of plush breeches which he wore into the place, and which he seems to have put off on being confined to his bed, by the increased violence of a complicated disease. He next gave out a catalogue of religious books, which must be brought together and burned, as unsafe in the hands of the people. March 6, in the afternoon, all things being ready, his followers carried a quantity of books to the wharf and burned them, singing around the pile, 'Hallelujah,' and 'Glory to God,' and declaring that, as the smoke of those books ascended up in their presence, so the smoke of the torment of such of their authors as died in the same belief, was now ascending in hell. Among the authors were Beveridge, Flavel, Drs. Increase Mather, Colman, and Sewall, and that fervid revivalist, Jonathan Parsons of Lyme. The next day, more books were burned, but one of the party persuaded the other to save the clothes.

This is the last recorded outbreak of Davenport's fanaticism. From this time, he disappears from the publications of the day, till the summer of 1744, when he published his 'Retractions' of his errors."[36]

Exhibit Two: James Davenport's "Retractions" of 1744

"Although I do not question at all, but there is great reason to bless God for a glorious and wonderful work of his power and grace in the edification of his children, and the conviction and conversion of numbers in New England, in the neighboring governments and several other parts, within a few years past; and believe that the lord hath favored me, though most unworthy, with several others of his servants, in granting special assistance and success; the glory of all which be given to Jehovah, to whom alone it belongs:

"Yet, after frequent meditation and desires that I might be enabled to apprehend things justly, and, I hope I may say, mature consideration, I am now fully convinced and persuaded that several appendages to this glorious work are no essential parts thereof, but of a different and contrary nature and tendency; which appendages I have been in the time of the work very industrious in, and instrumental of promoting, by a misguided zeal: being further much influenced in the affair by the false Spirit; which, unobserved by me, did (as I have been brought to see since) prompt me to unjust apprehensions and misconduct in several articles; which have been great blemishes to the work of God, very grievous to some of God's children, no less ensnaring and corrupting to others of them, a sad means of many persons questioning the work of God, concluding and appearing against it, and of the hardening of multitudes in their sins, and an awful occasion of the enemies blaspheming the right ways of the Lord; and withal very offensive to that God, before whom I would lie in the dust, prostrate in deep humility and repentance on this account, imploring pardon for the Mediator's sake, and thankfully accepting the tokens thereof.

---

[36] From Joseph Tracy, *The Great Awakening* (Edinburgh: The Banner of Truth Trust, 1842) 248-249.

"The articles, which I especially refer to, and would in the most public manner retract, and warn others against, are these which follow, viz.

"I. The method I used, for a considerable time, with respect to some, yea many ministers in several parts, in openly exposing such as I feared or thought unconverted, in public prayer or otherwise; herein making my private judgment, (in which also I much suspect I was mistaken in several instances, and I believe also that my judgment concerning several was formed rashly and upon very slender grounds,) I say, making my private judgment, the ground of public actions or conduct; offending, as I apprehend (although in the time of it, ignorantly) against the ninth commandment, and such other passages of Scripture as are similar; yea, I may say, offending against the laws both of justice and charity: which laws were further broken,

"II. By my advising and urging to such separations from those ministers whom I treated as above, as I believe may be justly called rash, unwarrantable, and of sad and awful tendency and consequence. And here I would ask the forgiveness of those ministers, whom I have injured in both these articles.

"III. I confess I have been much led astray by following impulses or impressions as a rule of conduct, whether they came with or without a text of Scripture; and my neglecting, also, duly to observe the analogy of Scripture. I am persuaded this was a great means of corrupting my experiences and carrying me off from the word of God, and a great handle, which the false Spirit has made use of with respect to a number, and me especially.

"IV. I believe, further, that I have done much hurt to religion, by encouraging private persons to a ministerial and authoritative kind or method of exhorting; which is particularly observable in many, such being much puffed up and falling into the snare of the devil, whilst many others are thus directly prejudiced against the work.

"I have reason to be deeply humbled that I have not been duly careful to endeavour to remove or prevent prejudice, (where I now believe I might then have done it consistently with duty,) which appeared remarkable in the method I practiced, of singing with others in the streets, in societies frequently.

"I would also penitently confess and bewail my great stiffness in retaining these aforesaid errors a great while, and unwillingness to examine into them with any jealousy of their being errors, notwithstanding the friendly counsels and cautions of real friends, especially in the ministry.

"Here may properly be added a paragraph or two, taken out of a letter from me to Mr Barber at Georgia; a true copy of which I gave consent, should be published lately at Philadelphia: '——I would add to what brother T---- hath written on the awful affair of books and clothes at New-London, which affords grounds of deep and lasting humiliation; I was, to my shame be it spoken, the ringleader in that horrid action; I was, my dear brother, under the powerful influence of the false Spirit, almost one whole day together, and part of several days. The Lord showed me afterwards that the spirit I was then acted by, was in its operations void of true inward peace, laying the greatest stress on externals, neglecting the heart, full of impatience, pride and arrogance; although I thought, in the time of it, that it was the Spirit of God in an high degree; awful indeed! my body, especially my leg much disordered at the same time (I had the long fever on me and the cankry humour raging at once), which Satan and my evil heart might make some handle of.'

"And now may the holy, wise and good God, be pleased to guard and secure me against such errors for the future, and stop the progress of those, whether ministers or people, who have been corrupted by my words or example in any of the above mentioned particulars; and, if it be his holy will, bless this public recantation to this purpose. And O! may he grant, withal, that such as by reason of the aforesaid errors and misconduct, have entertained unhappy prejudices against Christianity in general, or the late glorious work of God in particular, may, by this account, learn to distinguish the appendage from the substance or essence, that which is vile and odious, from that which is precious, glorious and divine, and thus be entirely and happily freed from all those prejudices referred to, and this, in infinite mercy through Jesus Christ: and to these requests, may all God's children, whether ministers or others say, amen.

"James Davenport.

"July 28. 1744.

"P.S. Inasmuch as a number, who have fallen in with and promoted the aforesaid errors and misconduct, and are not altered in their minds, may be prejudiced against this Recantation, by a supposition or belief, that I came into it by reason of desertion or dullness and deadness in religion, it seems needful, therefore, to signify, what I hope I may say without boasting, and what I am able, through pure rich grace, to speak with truth and freedom, that for some months in the time of my coming to the abovesaid conclusions and retractions, and since I have come through grace to them; I have been favored, a great part of the time, with a sweet calm and serenity of soul and rest in God, and sometimes with special and remarkable refreshments of soul, and these more free from corrupt mixtures than formerly. Glory to God alone. J. D."[37]

Exhibit Three: Edwards View of Davenport's "Retractions"

"Mr. [James] Davenport is truly very much altered; I am affected to see the happy alteration and change in him; he is quite another man. It has been moving to me to see the grace of God in so subduing, humbling, and enlightening him. He really shows an excellent spirit, much to the honor and glory of God; and I believe he is now much fuller of the Spirit of God than he was in years past, when he seemed to have such a constant series of high elevations and raptures. I think he is now fully satisfied in his duty in making a public, humble, and suitable recantation and confession of his great errors, that have been of such extensive and extremely hurtful consequence to the interest of religion. I cannot but believe that, notwithstanding all the insults which his humble retractions may be the occasions of among a generation of vipers, that yet they will be of great service to religion, and will open the door for his being now truly very serviceable by his preaching, in many places in New England, and especially there where he has done most hurt."[38]

---

[37] From Tracy, *The Great Awakening*, 249-252. In his remorse and concern that his earlier "misguided zeal" would have a continuing negative effect on his followers and the church of Christ in general, Davenport had his "Retractions" published.
[38] From a letter to Eleazar Wheelock, in Jonathan Edwards, *Letters and Personal Writings*, ed. George S. Claghorn, vol. 16 of *The Works of Jonathan Edwards* (New Haven: Yale University Press, 1998), 145-146.

SESSION THREE

Definition, Nature, Importance, and Scripture Support of Religious Affections

Suggested Reading:

- *The Religious Affections*, Banner of Truth, 21-53; or
- *The Religious Affections,* Yale University Press, 93-124.

I. **The Essence of True Christianity**[39]

"Whom having not seen, ye love; in whom, though now ye see him not, yet believing, ye rejoice with joy unspeakable and full of glory"[40] 1 Peter 1:8.

A) The essence of true religion is revealed by persecution.

"The apostle observes how true religion...under persecution, was manifested to be true religion, and eminently appeared in the genuine beauty and amiableness of true religion."[41]

In other words, persecution and suffering stripped away the dross and exposed the heart of "true religion."

B) The essence of true religion consists of love to Christ and joy in Christ.

C) *Therefore,* "true religion, in great part, consists in the affections."[42]

II. **The Nature and Definition of Religious Affections**[43]

A) A short definition of affections

"The affections are no other than the more vigorous and sensible exercises of the inclination and will of the soul."[44]

B) Affections and the faculties of the soul

---

[39] BT, 21-23; Yale, 93-95.
[40] 1 Peter 1:8, quoted in BT, 21; Yale, 93.
[41] BT, 22; Yale, 94.
[42] BT, 27; Yale, 99.
[43] BT, 23-27; Yale, 95-99.
[44] BT, 24; Yale, 96.

1) The soul consists of two faculties:[45]

   a) *Understanding*: "that by which it is capable of perception and speculation"

   b) *Inclination*: "that by which the soul is inclined...or averse" to that which it perceives.[46]

   i) With "respect to the *actions* that are determined and governed by it [the inclination], is called the *will*."

   All actions are determined by the will or inclination. We do what we *will* to do, or are *inclined* to do.[47]

   ii) With respect to the *mind*, the inclination "is often called the *heart*."

   For example, the heart of the unsaved sinner is inclined toward evil, and insofar as his or her thoughts are concerned, is said to have an evil heart. When we are saved, we are given a "new heart" and are progressively transformed "by the renewing of our minds" (Romans 12:2).

   Note: "Mind" and "heart" are often synonymous in Scripture, though Scripture does speak of a kind of knowledge that is merely intellectual and not of the "heart." In contemporary vernacular we sometimes distinguish "head" and "heart" knowledge, indicating something can be known intellectually without a more intimate spiritual knowledge. For instance, to know about God and to know and love Him intimately are different types of knowledge. For Edwards, a kind of intellectual ("notional") knowledge without "heart" knowledge is possible, but true spiritual heart knowledge always includes intellectual knowledge.

2) The *affections* as they relate to the *heart*

   Edwards distinguishes the *heart* and the *affections* in terms of degree, only, as affections are the more "vigorous and sensible" exercises of the heart. Any and all acts of the will are governed, prompted, and initiated by an inclination of the will (in this sense no acts of the will are uncaused), for we choose what we are inclined to choose. "But all the actings of the inclination and will, in all our common

---

[45] BT, 24; Yale, 96.
[46] BT, 24; Yale, 96.
[47] For Edwards, people do not choose to act against their will. For one, such would be a contradiction by definition, for Edwards defines the will as "that by which the mind chooses anything," thus doing something against one's will would be choosing something against one's choice. The same applies to coercion. For instance, when faced with the choice of giving a thief one's wallet or being shot, one will choose the option to which one is more favorably inclined. If one's will to live is greater than one's will to keep one's wallet (though the wallet will likely be lost in any event), one will *willingly* choose to forfeit the wallet. To give the wallet to the thief is an act of the will, as losing it to avoid bodily harm or death was preferable to keeping it and facing bodily harm or death. In this sense, all acts are willing acts. Jonathan Edwards, *Freedom of the Will*, ed. Paul Ramsey, *The Works of Jonathan Edwards*, vol. 1 (New Haven: Yale University Press, 1957), 137-140.

actions of life, are not ordinarily called affections."[48] The love of a mother toward her child is an "affection," whereas a mere preference of a blue versus a white dress is not.

III. Scriptural Evidence of the Centrality and Importance of Religious Affections to the Christian Life[49]

A) God requires earnest and fervent followers of Him.

Romans 12:2
Deuteronomy 6:4-5
Revelation 3:16
Matthew 10:37

B) The affections are the wellspring of human actions.

"Such is man's nature that he is very inactive, any otherwise than he is influenced by some affection, either love or hatred, desire, hope, fear, or some other."[50]

"He that has doctrinal knowledge and speculation only, without affection, never is engaged in the business of religion."[51]

Note: Edwards is not here de-emphasizing doctrinal knowledge (knowledge of the Word of God). He believed that Scripture, applied to the heart by the Holy Spirit, to be God's primary means of moving the affections. He is merely stating that head knowledge apart from heart knowledge will not generate true Christian works.

C) No considerable change in a life is possible apart from a change in one's affections.

"Never was a natural man engaged earnestly to seek his salvation; never were any such brought to cry after wisdom, and lift up their voice for understanding, and to wrestle with God in prayer for mercy; and never was one humbled and brought to the foot of God, from anything that ever he heard or imagined of his own unworthiness and deserving of God's displeasure; nor was ever one induced to fly for refuge unto Christ, while his heart remained unaffected."[52]

D) "The holy Scriptures do everywhere place religion very much in the affections; such as fear, hope, love, hatred, desire, joy, sorrow, gratitude, compassion, and zeal."[53]

1) Fear

"The fear of God is a great part of true godliness, hence true godliness in general, is very commonly called by the name of *the fear of God*."[54]

---

[48] BT, 26; Yale, 97.
[49] BT, 27-48; Yale, 99-119.
[50] BT, 29; Yale, 101.
[51] BT, 30; Yale, 101.
[52] BT, 30-31; Yale, 102.
[53] BT, 31; Yale, 102.
[54] BT, 31; Yale, 103.

2) Hope

> 1 Peter 1:3: "Blessed be the God and Father of our Lord Jesus Christ, which according to his abundant mercy, hath begotten us again unto a lively hope by the resurrection of Jesus Christ from the dead."

> Psalm 33:18
> Psalm 146:5
> Psalm 147:11
> Jeremiah 42:7
> Romans 8:24
> 1 Corinthians 13:13
> 1 Thessalonians 5:8

3) Love

> "The Scriptures place religion very much in the affection of *love*, in love to God and the Lord Jesus Christ, and love to the people of God, and to mankind. The texts in which this is manifest, both in the Old Testament and New, are innumerable."[55]

4) Hate

> Psalm 97:10a: "Ye that love the Lord, hate evil."
> Psalm 119:104b: "I hate every false way."
> Psalm 139:21: "Do not I hate them, O Lord, that hate thee?"
> Proverbs 8:13a: "The fear of the Lord is to hate evil."

5) Desire, longing for God

> Psalm 27:4: "One thing have I desired of the Lord, that will I seek after; that I may dwell in the house of the Lord all the days of my life, to behold the beauty of the Lord, and to inquire in his temple."

> Psalm 42:1-2: "As the hart [deer] panteth after the water brooks, so panteth my soul after Thee, O God; my soul thirsteth for God, for the living God: when shall I come and appear before God?"

> Psalm 63:1-2
> Psalm 84:1-2
> Psalm 119:20
> Psalm 73:25
> 143:6-7
> Isaiah 26:8

6) Joy

> Psalm 33:1: "Rejoice in the Lord, O ye righteous."

---

[55] BT, 32; Yale, 103.

Psalm 37:4: "Delight thyself also in the Lord; and he shall give thee the desires of thine heart."

Psalm 97:12
Matthew 5:12
Philippians 3:1
Philippians 4:4
1 Thessalonians 5:16

7) Sorrow, brokenness of heart

Psalm 34:18: "The Lord is near to the brokenhearted, and saves those who are crushed in spirit."

Psalm 51:17: "The sacrifices of God are a broken spirit; a broken and a contrite heart, O God, Thou wilt not despise."

Matthew 5:4: "Blessed are they that mourn; for they shall be comforted."

Psalm 51:17
Isaiah 57:15
Isaiah 66:2

8) Gratitude

"This being so much spoken of in the book of Psalms, and other parts of the holy Scriptures, I need not mention particular texts."[56]

9) Compassion and mercy

Matthew 5:7: "Blessed are the merciful, for they shall obtain mercy."

Colossians 3:12: "Put ye on, as the elect of God, holy and beloved, bowels of mercies, kindness, humbleness of mind, meekness, longsuffering patience."

Psalm 37:21, 26
Proverbs 14:31
Isaiah 57:1

10) Zeal

Titus 2:14: "[Christ Jesus] Who gave Himself for us, that He might redeem us from all iniquity, and purify unto himself a peculiar people, zealous of good works."

Revelation 3:15ff.

---

[56] BT, 34; Yale, 105.

E) Love is the foremost affection and the fountain of all affections.

    Matthew 22:37-40
    Romans 13:8-10

F) The Religion of the great saints of the Bible consisted in holy affections.

    1) David

    "Those holy songs of his he has there left us are nothing else but the expressions and breathings of devout and holy affections; such as an humble and fervent love to God, admiration of His glorious perfections and wonderful works, earnest desires, thirstings, and pantings of soul after God, delight and joy in God, a sweet and melting gratitude to God for His great goodness, a holy exultation and triumph of soul in the favour, sufficiency, and faithfulness of God, his love to and delight in the saints, the excellent of the earth, his great delight in the Word and ordinances of God, his grief for his own and the others' sins, and his fervent zeal for God and against the enemies of God and his church."[57]

    2) Paul

        Philippians 3:1-14
        2 Corinthians 2:4
        2 Corinthians 5:14
        2 Corinthians 6:11-13
        2 Corinthians 7:9-10

    3) John

        1 John 4:7-12
        3 John 2-4

G) The ministry of Christ was characterized by holy affections.

"He was the greatest instance of ardency, vigour and strength of love, to both God and man, that ever was."[58]

Mark 3:4-5
Luke 7:13
Luke 13:34
Luke 19:41-44
John 2:13-17
John 11:35-38

---

[57] BT, 37; Yale, 108.
[58] BT, 40; Yale, 111.

H) The religion of heaven consists in holy affections.

"The way to learn the true nature of anything is to go where that thing is to be found in its purity and perfection."[59]

Psalm 16:11
Isaiah 35:10

I) The nature and design of the duties that God has appointed show that true religion lies substantially in holy affections.

1) Prayer

"It is manifest we are not appointed in this duty to declare God's perfections, His majesty, holiness, goodness, and all-sufficiency, and our meanness, emptiness, dependence, and unworthiness, and our wants and desires, to inform God of these things, or to incline His heart, and prevail with Him to be willing to show us mercy; but suitably to affect our own hearts with the things we express, and so to prepare us to receive the blessings we ask."[60]

2) Praise

"And the duty of singing praises to God seems to be appointed wholly to excite and express religious affections. No other reason can be assigned why we should express ourselves to God in verse rather than in prose, and do it with music, but only that such is our nature and frame that these things have a tendency to move our affections."[61]

3) The "sacraments"

"God, considering our frame, hath not only appointed that we should be told of the great things of the gospel, and of the redemption of Christ, and instructed in them by His Word; but also that they should be, as it were, exhibited to our view, in sensible representations in the sacraments, the more to affect us with them."[62]

4) Preaching

"God hath appointed a particular and lively application of His Word to men in the preaching of it, as a fit means to affect sinners with the importance of the things of religion, and their own misery and necessity of a remedy, and the glory and sufficiency of a remedy provided; and to stir up the pure minds of the saints, and quicken their affections, by often bringing the great things of religion to their remembrance, and setting them before them in their proper colours, though they know them, and have been fully instructed in them already, 2 Pet. 1:12, 13. And, particularly, to promote those two affections in them which are spoken of in the text, love and joy."[63]

---

[59] BT, 43; Yale, 114.
[60] BT, 43-44; Yale, 114-115.
[61] BT, 44; Yale, 115.
[62] BT, 44; Yale, 115.
[63] BT, 44-45; Yale, 115-116.

J) That hardness of heart is sin is evidence that true religion lies in the affection of the heart

> Mark 3:5: "He looked round about on them with anger, being grieved for the hardness of their hearts."

> Ezekiel 3:7: "But the house of Israel will not hearken unto thee; for they will not hearken unto me: for all the house of Israel are impudent and hard-hearted."

> Ezekiel 11:19

IV. Implications for Proper Theology and Christian Living[64]

A) To reject affections as part of true Christianity is incorrect.

> "For although to true religion there must indeed be something else besides affection, yet true religion consists so much in the affections that there can be no true religion without them. He who has no religious affection is in a state of spiritual death, and is wholly destitute of the powerful, quickening, saving influences of the Spirit of God upon His heart. As there is no true religion where there is nothing else but affection, so there is no true religion where there is no religious affection. As, on the one hand, there must be light in the understanding as well as an affected fervent heart; where there is heat without light, there can be nothing divine or heavenly in that heart; so, on the other hand, where there is a kind of light without heat, a head stored with notions and speculations, with a cold and unaffected heart, there can be nothing divine in that light; that knowledge is no true spiritual knowledge of divine things."[65]

B) That which moves the religious affections is to be desired.

> "Such books, and such a way of preaching the word, and administering the ordinances, and such a way of worshipping God in prayer, and singing praises, is much to be desired, as have a tendency deeply to affect the hearts."[66]

> Note: Edwards must be read in the context of his day. He often read his sermons, usually two hours long, in a manner that many today would consider staid and dull. In desiring that which moved the heart, Edwards was no advocate of emotional manipulation: "Indeed there may be such means as may have a great tendency to stir up the passions of weak and ignorant persons, and yet have no great tendency to benefit their souls: for though they may have a tendency to excite affections, they may have little or none to excite gracious affections, or any affections tending to grace."[67]

C) If true religion lies much in the affections; we have reason to be ashamed before God.

> "How common is it among mankind, that their affections are much more exercised and engaged in other matters than in religion! In things which concern men's worldly interest, their outward delights, their honour and reputation, and their natural relations,

---

[64] BT, 48-53; Yale, 119-124.
[65] BT, 49-50; Yale, 120.
[66] BT, 50-51; Yale, 121.
[67] BT, 51; Yale, 122.

they have their desires eager, their appetites vehement, their love warm and affectionate, their zeal ardent; in these things their hearts are tender and sensible, easily moved, deeply impressed, much concerned, very sensibly affected, and greatly engaged; much depressed in grief at losses, and highly raised with joy at worldly successes and prosperity. But how insensible and unmoved are most men about the great things of another world! How dull are their affections! How heavy and hard their hearts in these matters! Here their love is cold, their desires languid, their zeal low, and their gratitude small. How they can sit and hear of the infinite height, and depth, and length, and breadth of the love of God in Christ Jesus, of His giving His infinitely dear son, to be offered up a sacrifice for the sins of men, and of the unparalleled love of the innocent, and holy, and tender Lamb of God, manifested in his dying agonies, his bloody sweat, his loud and bitter cries, and bleeding heart, and all this for enemies, to redeem them from deserved, eternal burnings, and to bring to unspeakable and everlasting joy and glory--and yet be cold and heavy, insensible and regardless! Where are our exercises of our affections proper, if not here?"[68]

"If we ought ever to exercise our affections at all, then they ought to be exercised about those objects which are most worthy of them. But is there anything which Christians can find in heaven or earth so worthy to be the objects of their admiration and love, their earnest and longing desires, their hope, and their rejoicing, and their fervent zeal, as those things that are held forth to us in the gospel of Jesus Christ? In which not only are things declared most worthy to affect us, but they are exhibited in the most affecting manner. The glory and beauty of the blessed Jehovah, which is most worthy in itself to be the object of our admiration and love, is there exhibited in the most affecting manner that can be conceived of, as it appears shining in all its luster in the face of an incarnate, infinitely loving, meek, compassionate, dying Redeemer. All the virtues of the Lamb of God, His humility, patience, meekness, submission, obedience, love and compassion, are exhibited to our view in a manner the most tending to move our affections of any that can be imagined; as they all had their greatest trial, and their highest exercise, and so their brightest manifestation, when He was in the most affecting circumstances; even when He was under His last sufferings, those unutterable and unparalleled sufferings He endured form his tender love and pity to us. There also the hateful nature of our sins is manifested in the most affecting manner possible: as we see the dreadful effects of them in what our Redeemer, who undertook to answer for us, suffered for them. And there we have the most affecting manifestation of God's hatred of sin, and His wrath and justice in punishing it; as we see His justice in the strictness and inflexibleness of it; and His wrath in its terribleness, in so dreadfully punishing our sins, in One who was infinitely dear to Him, and loving to us. So has God disposed things in the affair of our redemption, and in His glorious dispensations, revealed to us in the gospel, as though every thing were purposely contrived in such a manner as to have the greatest possible tendency to reach our hearts in the most tender part, and move our affections most sensibly and strongly. How great cause have we therefore to be humbled to the dust that we are no more affected!"[69]

---

[68] BT, 51-52; Yale, 122-123.
[69] BT, 52-53; Yale, 123-124.

Questions and Points for Discussion

1) Do we find our own affections moved as much by Christ and the precious things of the Gospel as by the things of this world?

2) In the New Testament, the mind and the heart are often used interchangeably. Does Edwards' explanation of the nature of "gracious" religious affections help us to understand why?

3) What can move the heart of saints more than that which is the most excellent and lovely?

4) How is correct theology foundational to God-honoring religious affections?

5) What produced the gracious affections of David and the apostles?

6) Would Edwards agree with many of the techniques utilized today to move the affections? Why or why not?

PART TWO

Uncertain Signs that Religious Affections are the Work of God in a True Believer

SESSION FOUR

Suggested Reading:

- *The Religious Affections*, Banner of Truth, 54-64; or
- *The Religious Affections*, Yale University Press, 127-137.

Introduction

"We ought not to reject and condemn all affections as though true religion did not at all consist in affection; so, on the other hand, we ought not to approve of all, as though every one that was religiously affected had true grace, and was therein the subject of the saving influences of the Spirit of God."[70]

In part two of *the Religious Affections*, Edwards analyzes twelve signs identified by both proponents and opponents of the Awakening in support for their view. On the one hand, some of the more vigorous opponents of the Awakening viewed each of these twelve signs as definite evidence that the religious affections producing them were not of God.[71] In contrast, many supporters of the Awakening viewed the same signs as conclusive evidence of a true work of God.

<u>Illustrated</u>:

"None of God"   **"All of God"**

1. Religious fervor and zeal
2. Great bodily effects
3. Abundant religious talk
4. Apparent supernatural origin of affections
5. That affections come accompanied by Scripture
6. The presence of love
7. The presence of many different types of affections
8. That joys follow convictions of conscience
9. Zealous religious activity
10. Abundant praise
11. Great assurance of salvation
12. Great moving testimonies

---

[70] BT, 54; Yale, 127.
[71] With the exception of sign six. The presence of love was not viewed by opponents of the Awakening as evidence that the affections associated with it were not of God.

Uncertain Signs

Sign I: Religious Fervor or Zeal

A) As evidence of gracious and holy affections[72]

"If it be, as has been proved, that true religion lies very much in religious affections, then it follows that, if there be a great deal of true religion, there will be great religious affections; if true religion in the hearts of men be raised to a great height, divine and holy affections will be raised to a great height."[73]

"Love is an affection, but will any Christian say, men ought not to love God and Jesus Christ in a high degree? And will any say, we ought not to have a very great hatred of sin, and a very deep sorrow for it? Or that we ought not to exercise a high degree of gratitude to God for the mercies we receive of Him, and the great things He has done for the salvation of fallen men? Or that we should not have very great and strong desires after God and holiness? Is there any who will profess that his affections in religion are great enough, and will say, 'I have no cause to be humbled, that I am no more affected with the things of religion than I am; I have no reason to be ashamed, that I have no great exercises of love to God and sorrow for sin, and gratitude for the mercies which I have received. Who is there that will bless God that he is affected enough with what he has read and heard of the wonderful love of God to worms and rebels, in giving His only begotten Son to die for them, and with the dying love of Christ; and will pray that he may not be affected with them in any higher degree?"[74]

"We find the most eminent saints in Scripture often professing high affections," such as the Psalmist (David), the Apostle Paul, John the Baptist, the woman who anointed the body of Jesus, "the church in her future happy seasons," and the "saints and angels in heaven."[75]

Psalm 21:1: "The king shall joy in thy strength, O Lord, and in thy salvation how greatly shall he rejoice."

Psalm 68:3: "Let the righteous be glad: let them rejoice before God; yea, let them exceedingly rejoice."

Psalm 119:136: "Rivers of waters run down mine eyes, because they keep not thy law."

Psalm 63:3-7
Psalm 89:15-16
Zechariah 9:9
John 3:29

B) As evidence of natural affections

"On the other hand, it is no evidence that religious affections are of a spiritual and gracious nature, because they are great....There are religious affections which are very high that are not spiritual and saving."[76]

---

[72] Edwards uses "gracious and holy affections" to refer to affections generated by the Holy Spirit's work in the heart of a true believer.
[73] BT, 54-55; Yale, 127.
[74] BT, 55; Yale, 127-128.
[75] BT, 56-57; Yale, 128-130.

"So the children of Israel were greatly affected with God's mercy to them when they had seen how wonderfully He wrought for them at the Red Sea, where they sang God's praise; though they soon forgat his works."[77]

In the short span of a week, the shouts of "hosanna" at Christ's entry into Jerusalem turned to "crucify" as He stood before Pilate.[78]

Sign II: Great Physical Affects on the Body

As affections affect us physically, and affections can be natural or spiritual, then the cause of great physical affects (fainting, shaking, sweating, exhaustion, etc.) can be either natural or spiritual.

A) As evidence of natural affections

"Great affects on the body certainly are no sure evidences that affections are spiritual; for we see that such effects oftentimes arise from great affections about temporal things, and when religion is no way concerned in them."[79]

B) As evidence of gracious and holy affections

"I know of no reason why a being affected with a view of God's glory should not cause the body to faint, as well as being affected with a view of Solomon's glory."[80]

Psalm 119:120: "My flesh trembleth for fear of Thee."

Habakkuk 3:16: "When I heard, my belly trembled: my lips quivered at the voice: rottenness entered into my bones, and I trembled in myself."

Revelation 1:17: "And when I saw Him [Christ in His glory], I fell at His feet as dead."

Daniel 10:6-9

C) As inconclusive evidence of natural or gracious and holy affections

"Universal experience shows that the exercise of the affections has in a special manner a tendency to some sensible effect upon the body....and the more vigorous their exercise...the greater will be the effect on the body. Very great and strong exercises of the affections have great affects on the body. And therefore, seeing there are very great affections, both common and spiritual, it is not to be wondered at that great effects on the body should arise from both these kinds of affections. And consequently these effects are no signs that the affections they arise from are of one kind or the other."[81]

---

[76] BT, 57-58; Yale, 130.
[77] BT, 58; Yale, 130-131.
[78] BT, 58-59; Yale, 131. See Exodus 24:3, 32:1; and Matthew 9:8, 30-33; 12:23; 15:30-31; 21:9-11; 27:17-23 for a picture of great religious affections that are later seen to be from something other than a saving love to God.
[79] BT, 59; Yale, 132.
[80] BT, 60; Yale, 132.
[81] BT, 59; Yale, 132.

Sign III: Fluent, Fervent, and Abundant Religious Talk

"There are many persons who, if they see this in others, are greatly prejudiced against them. Their being so full of talk is with them a sufficient ground to condemn them as Pharisees and ostentatious hypocrites. On the other hand, there are many who, if they see this effect in any, are very ignorantly and imprudently forward at once to determine that they are the true children of God, and are under the saving influences of His Spirit, and speak of it as a great evidence of a new creature...for this is but the religion of the mouth and of the tongue, and what is in the Scripture represented by the leaves of a tree, which, though the tree ought not to be without them, yet are nowhere given as an evidence of the goodness of the tree."[82]

A) As evidence of gracious and holy affections

To speak fluently, fervently, and abundantly regarding one's greatest love is entirely appropriate, "for out of the abundance of the heart the mouth speaketh." "It is very much the nature of the affections, of whatever kind they be, and whatever objects they are exercised about, if they are strong, to dispose persons to be very much in speaking of that which they are affected."[83]

B) As evidence of natural affections

"A Pharisee's trumpet shall be heard to the town's end, when simplicity walks through the town unseen. Hence a man will sometimes covertly commend himself (and *myself* ever comes in), and tells you a long story of conversion; and a hundred to one if some lie or other slip not out with it. Why, the secret meaning is, *I pray admire me*, and *Pray think what a broken-hearted Christian am I*."[84]

"O reader, if thy heart were right with God, and thus didst not cheat thyself with a vain profession, thou wouldst have frequent business with God which thou wouldst be loth thy dearest friend, or the wife of thy bosom, should be privy to….Religion doth not lie open to all, to the eyes of men. Observed duties maintain our credit; but secret duties maintain our life."[85]

"A person may be over-full of talk of his own experiences, commonly falling upon it everywhere and in all companies; and when it is so, it is rather a dark sign than a good one."[86]

Edwards gives the multitudes following John the Baptist and then Christ during His earthly ministry as examples of the effects of natural affections, asking: "But what did these things come to in the greater part of them?"[87]

C) Inconclusive as evidence of natural or gracious and holy affections

"That persons are disposed to be abundant in talking of things of religion may be from a good cause, and it may be from a bad one."[88]

---

[82] BT, 62-63; Yale, 135-136.
[83] BT, 63; Yale, 136.
[84] Shepard, *Parable of the Ten Virgins*, 284; quoted in BT, 64-65, footnote; Yale, 137, footnote 3.
[85] Flavel, *Touchstone of Sincerity*. *Works* Vol. 5, 520; quoted in BT, 65, footnote; Yale, 137, footnote 3.
[86] BT, 64; Yale, 137.
[87] BT, 63-64; Yale, 136-137.
[88] BT, 63; Yale, 136.

Questions and Points for Discussion

1) Ecstatic experience and bodily effects are the desired effect or evidence of heightened religious experience in many pagan religions. How do Edwards' arguments apply here?

2) How is the life of the apostle Paul prior to his conversion illustrative of Edwards' argument concerning fervor and zeal?

3) Is zeal *always* something that is outward and visible to others?

4) What are some possible reasons why someone without saving faith in Christ would speak abundantly about Christ?

5) How do Matthew 6:5-6 and James 1:19 relate to sign three? Do these verses teach us to *not* speak of Christ and the Gospel? What do they teach and how do they relate to Edwards' arguments?

6) How do you reconcile the many passages of Scripture that exhort us to speak abundantly about the glories of Christ and the Gospel, as evidenced by the ministries of the Apostles and Christ Himself, with passages that exhort us to be slow to speak and to not display our religiosity to be seen by others? How can we err on the side of not speaking enough or of speaking too much?

SESSION FIVE

Suggested Reading:

- *The Religious Affections,* Banner of Truth, 65-79; or
- *The Religious Affections,* Yale University Press, 138-151.

Sign IV: That Affections Seem To Be from an External Supernatural Source

Many experiencing highly elevated religious affections during the Great Awakening attributed their experience to "some extrinsic and supernatural power upon their minds."[89] Supposing the source of the experience to be outside themselves and produced by other than natural means, they concluded it must be from the Holy Spirit. Others believed the "manner of the Spirit of God is to co-operate in a silent, secret, and indiscernible way with the use of means, and our own endeavors; so that there is no distinguishing by sense between the influences of the Spirit of God and the natural operations of the faculties of our own minds."[90] On this basis they denied that the Holy Spirit could be the source of such "supernatural" experience. Edwards acknowledged the possibility of a natural or divine source, but viewed the seemingly supernatural source of the experience as inconclusive evidence for either explanation.

A) As evidence of gracious and holy affections

1) "If grace be indeed owing to the powerful and efficacious operation of an extrinsic agent, or divine efficient out of ourselves, why is it unreasonable to suppose it should seem to be so to them who are the subjects of it? Is it a strange thing that it should seem to be as it is?"[91]

   In other words, as God is supernatural it follows that His work in our life would appear as supernatural, as originating outside of ourselves.

2) Scripture compares God's work in the heart to things which can be accomplished by God only, that display His great power, such as being born again, raised from the dead, given sight, created anew, and "being brought out of nothing into being."[92]

   Ephesians 1:17-20

3) "It is God's manner, in the great works of His power and mercy which He works for His people, to order things so as to make His hand visible, and His power conspicuous, and men's dependence on Him most evident, that no flesh should glory in His presence."[93]

---

[89] BT, 65; Yale, 138.
[90] BT, 65; Yale, 138.
[91] BT, 66; Yale, 138-139.
[92] BT, 66; Yale, 139.
[93] BT, 67; Yale, 139-140.

Judges 7:2
Isaiah 2:11-17
1 Corinthians 1:27-29
2 Corinthians 4:7
2 Corinthians 12:9

Examples of the necessity and display of the power of God include the redemption of Israel from Egypt, Gideon, David and Goliath, the calling of the Gentiles, and the conversions in the New Testament.[94]

B) As evidence of natural affections

   1) The Spirit of God often works in secret and gradual ways.

   "The Spirit of God is very various in the manner and circumstances of His operations, and that sometimes He operates in a way more secret and gradual, and from smaller beginnings, than at others."[95]

   2) God has ordained human responsibility in the growth process.

   "For any to expect to receive the saving influences of the Spirit of God while they neglect a diligent improvement of the appointed means of grace [i.e., Bible study, prayer, et al], is unreasonable presumption."[96]

   3) Satan and demons influence us.

   "There are other spirits who have influence on the minds of men besides the Holy Ghost. We are directed not to believe every spirit, but to try the spirits whether they be of God. There are many false spirits, exceeding busy with men, who often transform themselves into angels of light, and do in many wonderful ways, with great subtlety and power, mimic the operation of the Spirit of God. And there are many of Satan's operations, which are very distinguishable from the voluntary exercises of men's own minds."[97]

   4) The Holy Spirit also works in common and non-saving ways.

   Hebrews 6:4-5

   5) While people can be susceptible to deceptive "impressions" upon their minds, some are more susceptible.

   "We see that such persons are liable to such impressions about temporal things; and there is equal reason why they should about spiritual things. As a person who is asleep has dreams that he is not the voluntary author of; so may such persons in like manner be the subjects of involuntary impressions when they are awake."[98]

---

[94] BT, 67; Yale 140.
[95] BT, 65; Yale, 138.
[96] BT, 65; Yale, 138.
[97] BT, 69; Yale, 141-142.
[98] BT, 69; Yale, 142.

Sign V: That Religious Affections Come with Texts of Scripture in the Mind

Some concluded that if great affections (such as fear, hope, joy, sorrow, and others) came with Scripture texts in their mind, the experience must be from God and be an indication of one's salvation. But there are other possible explanations.

A) Scripture is perfect, but it can be abused and misapplied.

   1) By Satan

   "And if Satan did presume, and was permitted to put Christ Himself in mind of texts of Scripture to tempt *Him*, what reason have we to determine that he dare not, or will not be permitted, to put wicked men in mind of tests of Scripture to tempt and deceive *them?*"[99]

   Matthew 4:1-11

   2) By false teachers

   "We see they have the free use of Scripture in every part of it: there is no text so precious and sacred but they are permitted to abuse it, to the eternal ruin of multitudes of souls; and there are no weapons they make use of with which they do more execution."[100]

   2 Peter 3:16

   3) By ourselves

   Matthew 7:21-23

Sign VI: The Presence of Love

Those opposing the Awakening did not view the presence of love as evidence against God's gracious work in the heart of a professing Christian. However, "there are some who suppose it is a good evidence that affections are from the sanctifying and saving influences of the Holy Ghost. Their argument is that Satan cannot love...whose very nature is enmity and malice," and as love "is the chief of the graces of God's Spirit, and the life, essence and sum of all true religion; and that by which we are most conformed to heaven, and most contrary to hell and the devil," its presence with religious affections confirms their source as God.[101]

But:

A) "The more excellent anything is, the more will be the counterfeits of it."[102]

   "Thus there are many more counterfeits of silver and gold than of iron and copper: there are many false diamonds and rubies, but who goes about to counterfeit common stones?"[103]

---

[99] BT, 71; Yale 144.
[100] BT, 72; Yale, 145.
[101] BT, 73; Yale, 146.
[102] BT, 73; Yale, 146.
[103] BT, 73; Yale 146.

"The subtlety of Satan, and men's deceitful hearts, are wont chiefly to be exercised in counterfeiting those that are in highest repute. So there are perhaps no graces that have more counterfeits than love and humility, these being virtues wherein the beauty of a true Christian does especially appear."[104]

B) There is a kind of religious love that is absent of saving grace.

Matthew 24:12-13: "And because iniquity shall abound, the love of many shall wax cold. But he that shall endure unto the end, the same shall be saved."

Ephesians 6:24: "Grace be with all them that love our Lord Jesus Christ in sincerity."

"There may be strong affections of this kind without saving grace; as there were in the Galatians towards the Apostle Paul, when they were ready to pluck out their eyes and give them to him; although the apostle expresses his fear that their affections were come to nothing, and that he had bestowed upon them labour in vain" (Galatians 4:11, 15).[105]

Sign VII: The Presence of Many Kinds of Religious Affections Accompanying Each Other

A) Counterfeits of all kinds of affections exist.

   1) Sorrow for sin

      Pharaoh (Exodus 9:27)

      Saul (1 Samuel 24:16-17; 26:1)

      Ahab (1 Kings 21:27)

      Israel in the wilderness (Numbers 14:39-41)

   2) Gratitude

      Israel following parting of Red Sea (Psalm 106:12ff)

   3) Joy

      "Stony-ground" hearers (Matthew 13:20)

      John the Baptist's followers (John 5:35)

   4) Zeal

      Jehu (2 Kings 10:16)

      Paul before conversion (Galatians 1:14; Philippians 3:6)

---

[104] BT, 73; Yale, 146.
[105] BT, 74-75; Yale, 147.

5) Love and the affections that flow from it

> "It is easy, from nature, and the nature of the affections, to give an account why, when one affection is raised very high, it should excite others; especially if the affection which is raised high be that of counterfeit love, as it was in the multitude who cried 'Hosanna.' This will naturally draw many other affections after it."[106]

> "As from true divine love flow all Christian affections, so from a counterfeit love in like manner naturally flow other false affections. In both cases, love is the foundation, and the other affections are the streams...if there be sweet water in the fountain, sweet water will thence flow out into those various channels; but if the water in the fountain be poisonous, then poisonous streams will flow out into all those channels."[107]

B) Deception can produce responses that appear identical to those produced by the Spirit of God in true believers.

"Suppose a person who has been for some time in great exercise and terror through fear of hell...on the brink of despair...is all at once delivered by being firmly made to believe, through some delusion of Satan, that God has pardoned him, and accepts him as the object of His dear love, and promises him eternal life....what various passions would naturally crowd at once, or one after another, into such a person's mind!...A person's heart on such an occasion should be raised up to the skies with transports of joy, and be filled with fervent affection to that imaginary God or Redeemer."[108]

Note: While one deceived into thinking he has been saved from the fires of hell may exhibit the identical outward appearance of joy, gratitude, and zeal as one truly saved, their hearts will be different. And though one falsely convinced he has been cured of terminal cancer may react in the same manner as someone who has truly been cured, the qualitative difference between affections produced by the Holy Spirit and those of the natural man is considerable. The difference may not be readily discernible to the outside observer, at least in the short run, but the difference is no less significant. This will become clear later in the study.

Questions and Points for Discussion

1) As with physical growth, spiritual growth is often imperceptible over short periods of time, but becomes evident over a longer span. For instance, how much have you grown spiritually in the last hour as compared to the last five years? Additionally many of God's ways are beyond our understanding (see John 3:5-8, Ecclesiastes 8:16-17, and Romans 11:33). Thus, is God's imperceptible work contradictory to God's purpose to display His power through His works? Why or why not?

---

[106] BT, 76; Yale, 149.
[107] BT, 78; Yale, 150-151.
[108] BT, 76-77; Yale, 149.

2) Many who were quite confident that their experiences during the Awakening were from God fell away from professing Christ when the excitement of the Awakening ceased. What does this say about the nature and source of their experience?

3) Can unbelievers be comforted or deluded into a false sense of security by a Scripture passage that does not apply to them? How do people know that the promises of blessing and not the promises of judgment apply to them? [this will be discussed at length under sign eleven below]

4) Do we ever enlist God to our defense when we want to rationalize our sin by picking and choosing selected Scriptures to suit our own ends?

5) God tells us that "he who trusts in his own heart is a fool" (Proverbs 28:26). Drawing upon Edwards' analysis, why? How does Jeremiah 17:9 relate to Proverbs 28:26?

6) If love is the spring of all other affections, and if the object and basis of one's love is not God, what does that say about the other affections that spring from that love?

SESSION SIX

Suggested Reading:

- *The Religious Affections*, Banner of Truth, 79-95; or
- *The Religious Affections*, Yale University Press, 151-167.

Sign VIII: That Joy and Comfort Follow Conviction and Mourning for Sin

A) Arguments that joy and comfort following conviction and mourning for sin is evidence of God's grace.

1) "Surely it cannot be unreasonable to suppose that, before God delivers persons from a state of sin and exposedness to eternal destruction, He should give them some considerable sense of the evil He delivers them from; that they may be delivered sensibly, and understand their own salvation, and know something of what God does for them."[109]

   In other words, as one saved passes from eternal condemnation before God into total forgiveness and new life, it follows that the experience be conviction of sin and despair followed by the joy of forgiveness and reconciliation to God, and that one should be sensible of this great transition. It is reasonable that experience corresponds with reality.

2) "It is God's manner of dealing with men, to 'lead them into a wilderness, before he speaks comfortably to them...' that they shall be brought into distress, and made to see their own helplessness and absolute dependence on His power and grace, before he appears to work any great deliverance for them."[110]

   Exodus 2:19, 23
   Leviticus 13:45
   Deuteronomy 8:2, 16
   Deuteronomy 32:36-37
   Matthew 15:22-28
   Mark 5:25-29
   Luke 8:43-44
   2 Corinthians 1:8-10

   Note: It was the consistent pattern of God's dealing with Israel that he brought them low in their sin through judgment, and subsequently restored them when they humbled themselves and repented of their sin.

---

[109] BT, 79; Yale, 152.
[110] BT, 79-80; Yale, 152.

3) God has often "manifested Himself in a way which was terrible, and then by those things that were comfortable."[111]

To Abraham: "And when the sun was going down, a deep sleep fell upon Abram; and, lo, an horror of great darkness fell upon him" (Genesis 15:12).

To Elijah (1 Kings 19:11-13)

To Moses (Hebrews 12:18-21)

To Daniel (Daniel 10)

To the Apostle John (Revelation 1:9ff.)

4) Scripture directly shows that conviction of conscience preceding comfort and joy is God's typical manner in salvation.[112]

Genesis 3:15
Psalm 72:6
Isaiah 32:2
Jeremiah 8:11
Matthew 3:7-10
Luke 15
Acts 2:36-41
Hebrews 6:18

B) Arguments to the contrary

1) Men can be terrified of hell with no conviction of their sin.

"Terror and a conviction of conscience are different things. For though convictions of conscience do often cause terror, yet they do not consist in it; and terrors do often arise from other causes."[113]

"Some persons that have frightful apprehensions of hell, a dreadful pit ready to swallow them up, and flames just ready to lay hold of them, and devils around them ready to seize them; who at the same time seem to have very little proper enlightenment of conscience really convincing them of their sinfulness of heart and life."[114]

2) "Men can be terrified by the devil."[115]

3) Some people are easily impressionable and excitable.

---

[111] BT, 81; Yale, 153-154.
[112] BT, 81-83; Yale, 154-155.
[113] BT, 83-84; Yale, 156.
[114] BT, 84; Yale, 156.
[115] BT, 84; Yale, 156.

"Some persons are of such a temper and frame that their imaginations are more strongly impressed with everything they are affected with than others; and the impression on the imagination reacts on the affection, and raises that still higher...til their affection is raised to a vast height."[116]

4) Some people do not grasp the true nature of sin.

"They tell of a dreadful load and sink of sin, a heap of black and loathsome filthiness within them; when, if the matter be carefully inquired into, they have not in view anything wherein the corruption of nature does truly exist."[117]

5) Even if there is the appearance of conviction and humiliation, such is not certain evidence that the "lights and comforts which follow are true and saving."[118]

   a) "As the devil can counterfeit all the saving operations and graces of the Spirit of God, so he can counterfeit those operations that are preparatory to grace" [such as conviction of sin].[119]

   "There are false humiliations and false submission, as well as false comforts."[120]

   "There is oftentimes in men who are terrified through fears of hell, a great appearance of their being brought off from their own righteousness, when they are not brought off from it in all ways, although they are in many ways that are more plain and visible. They have only exchanged some ways of trusting in their own righteousness for others that are more secret and subtle."[121] In other words, in becoming more subtle and sophisticated in self-righteousness, one can give the appearance of having repented of self-righteousness when there is no true repentance.

   "Oftentimes a great degree of discouragement, as to many things they used to depend upon, is taken for humiliation: and that is called a submission to God which is no absolute submission, but has some secret bargain in it that it is hard to discover."[122]

   b) If Satan can imitate the external appearance of the "effects of the Spirit of God," he can imitate their order.[123]

   c) No "certain rule" exists as to how far the Holy Spirit goes in convicting people of sin without actually saving them.[124]

---

[116] BT, 84; Yale, 157.
[117] BT, 85; Yale, 157.
[118] BT, 85; Yale, 157.
[119] BT, 86-87; Yale, 158-159.
[120] BT, 86; Yale, 158.
[121] BT, 87; Yale, 159.
[122] BT, 87; Yale, 159.
[123] BT, 87; Yale, 159.
[124] BT, 87-88; Yale, 159-160.

d) Experience shows that many seemingly converted in this manner subsequently fall away from the faith (such was frequently observed by ministers during the Great Awakenings).[125]

   i) The work of the Holy Spirit is mysterious and cannot be reduced to a series of steps or methods.

   "It is to be feared that some have gone too far towards directing the Spirit of the Lord, and marking out His footsteps for Him, and limiting Him to certain steps and methods. Experience plainly shows, that God's Spirit is unsearchable and untraceable, in some of the best Christians, in the method of His operations in their conversion."[126]

   Ecclesiastes 11:5: "Thou knowest not what is the way of the Spirit, or how the bones do grow in the womb of her that is with child; even so thou knowest not the works of God that worketh all."

   Isaiah 40:13: "Who hath directed the Spirit of the Lord, or being his counselor has taught Him?"

   Proverbs 25:2: "It is the glory of God to conceal a thing."

   ii) Over time, people tend to conform their conversion stories to the accepted standard.

   "At first, their experiences appear like a confused chaos, as Mr. Shepard expresses it: but then those passages of their experience are picked out, that have most of the appearance of such particular steps that are insisted on; and these are dwelt upon in the thoughts, and these are told of from time to time in the relation they give: these parts grow brighter and brighter in their view; and others, being neglected, grow more and more obscure; and what they have experienced is insensibly strained to bring all to an exact conformity to the scheme that is established."[127]

6) "We are often in Scripture expressly directed to try ourselves by the nature of the fruits of the Spirit; but nowhere by the Spirit's method of producing them."[128]

Sign IX: Great Time and Energy Spent in Religious Activity and Worship

A) As evidence of gracious and holy affections

The heart of the true saint delights in God, and therefore delights in God's Word, God's people, God's service, prayer, and worship.

---

[125] BT, 88; Yale, 160.
[126] BT, 89-90; Yale, 161-162.
[127] BT, 90; Yale, 162.
[128] BT, 90; Yale, 162.

Acts 2:46-47: "And they continuing daily with one accord in the temple, and breaking bread from house to house, did eat their meat with gladness and singleness of heart, praising God."

Psalm 26:8
Psalm 55:17
Psalm 135:3
Psalm 139:15
Psalm 147:1
Isaiah 52:7
Luke 2:37

B) As evidence of natural affections

1) The religion of hypocrisy often involves great displays of outward religious activity.[129]

   Isaiah 1:12-15
   Isaiah 58:4
   Ezekiel 33:31-32
   Mark 6:20
   John 5:35

2) Outward displays of great religious zeal and activity may be as much an evidence of someone trusting in their works for salvation as an evidence of the gracious work of God in the heart of a believer.[130]

   Examples: Religious ascetics such as recluses, hermits, and anchorites

Sign X: Abundant Praise to God

A) This point is an extension of the two previous points.

B) Instances where praise to God was not necessarily the manifestation of God's grace in the heart:

1) Mark 2:12: "And immediately he arose, took up his bed, and went forth before them all, insomuch that they were all amazed, and glorified God, saying, 'We never saw it on this fashion.'"

2) Matthew 15:31 "Insomuch that the multitude wondered when they saw the dumb to speak, the maimed to be whole, the lame to walk, and the blind to see: and they glorified the God of Israel."

3) Luke 6:15: "And he taught in their synagogues, being glorified of all."

4) Hosanna! Crucify!

---

[129] BT, 91-92; Yale, 163-164.
[130] BT, 92-93; Yale, 164-165.

Questions and Points for Discussion

1) What does it mean that there is a "qualitative" difference between the joy and gratitude produced by good news in the heart of an unbeliever and that of a believer?

2) When itinerant preachers of the Awakening went into churches and accused pastors of being unregenerate, how could they have positively known the spiritual state of the pastor? What could they have determined by the presence of any of the ten signs discussed thus far?

3) "Oftentimes a great degree of discouragement, as to many things they used to depend upon, is taken for humiliation: and that is called a submission to God which is no absolute submission, but has some secret bargain in it that it is hard to discover." What might some "secret bargains" be?

4) Is it possible to serve God too much? Why or why not?

5) Given Edwards' arguments, is it theologically possible (in principle) to have a stadium filled with people singing praises to God but have no believers present? Is it possible for an evangelical church to have an unbelieving pastor or worship leader? Why or why not?

6) Why did the crowds follow Jesus? What are some possible reasons why they praised Him?

SESSION SEVEN

Suggested Reading:

- *The Religious Affections*, Banner of Truth, 95-110; or
- *The Religious Affections*, Yale University Press, 167-181.

Sign XI: Great Assurance of One's Own Salvation

Some opponents of the Awakening argued that "persons are deluded if they pretend to be assured of their good estate, and to be carried beyond all doubting of the favour of God; supposing that there is no such thing to be expected in the church of God as a full and absolute assurance of hope."[131]

Note: Assurance is not eternal security. Eternal security is objective and unchanging truth, based upon clear statements of Scripture that say, once a child of God, always a child of God. Assurance is subjective, variable, and based on one's heartfelt knowledge or confidence that one is a child of God.

A) The Bible teaches assurance of salvation.

   1) The Old Testament teaches assurance.

"David, throughout the book of Psalms, almost everywhere speaks without any hesitancy, and in the most positive manner, of God as His God: glorying in Him as his Portion and Heritage, his Rock and Confidence, his Shield, Salvation, and High Tower, and the like."[132]

"God, in the plainest and most positive manner, revealed and testified his special favour to Noah, Abraham, Isaac, Jacob, Moses, Daniel, and others."[133]

Job 19:25: "I know that my Redeemer liveth, and that I shall see him for myself, and not another."

   2) The New Testament teaches assurance.

      a) Christ taught assurance.[134]

John 15:11: "These things have I spoken unto you, that my joy might remain in you, and that your joy might be full."

---

[131] BT, 95; Yale, 167.
[132] BT, 96; Yale, 167-168.
[133] BT, 96; Yale, 167.
[134] BT, 96-97; Yale, 168.

John 16:33: "These things I have spoken unto you, that in Me ye might have peace. In the world ye shall have tribulation: but be of good cheer, I have overcome the world."

John 17

b) The Epistles teach assurance.

Galatians 2:20
Philippians 1:21
2 Timothy 1:12
2 Timothy 4:7-8

c) The nature and purpose of the covenant of grace [the "new covenant"] is to give assurance.

"For so are all things ordered and contrived in that covenant, that every thing might be made sure on God's part....The promises are most full, and very often repeated, and various ways exhibited; and there are many witnesses and many seals; and God has confirmed His promises with an oath. God's declared design in all this is, that the heirs of the promises might have an undoubting hope and full joy, in an assurance of their future glory."[135]

Hebrews 6:17-18

d) Assurance can be attained.

1 Corinthians 2:12: "Now we have received, not the spirit of the world, but the Spirit who is of God; that we might know the things that are freely given to us by God."

1 John 2:3: "And hereby we do know that we know him, if we keep his commandments."

1 John 3:14: "We know we have passed from death unto life, because we love the brethren"

1 John 3:19: "Hereby we know that we are of the truth, and shall assure our hearts before him."

1 John 3:24: "Hereby we know that he abideth in us, by the Spirit which he hath given us."

1 John 4:13
1 John 5:2, 19

e) To not have assurance is unbecoming of Christians.

2 Corinthians 13:5: "Know ye not your own selves, how that Jesus Christ is in you, except you be reprobates?"

---

[135] BT, 97; Yale, 169.

3) Conclusion

It is "very unreasonable to determine that persons are hypocrites, and their affections wrong" because they have no fear of hell and do not doubt their salvation.[136]

B) Assurance may be false.

1) The self-righteous ("hypocrites") often have great assurance.

"You have, it may be, done and suffered many things in and for religion; you have excellent gifts and sweet comforts, a warm zeal for God, and high confidence of your integrity: all this may be right...but yet, it is possible it may be false. You have sometimes judged yourselves, and pronounced yourselves upright; but remember your final sentence is not yet pronounced by your Judge....*Things that are highly esteemed of men, are an abomination in the sight of God*: He seeth not as man seeth. Thy heart may be false, and thou not know it: yea, it may be false, and thou strongly confident of its integrity."[137]

"Some hypocrites are a great deal more confident than many saints."[138]

Example: The Pharisees (John 8:31-59)

2) The hypocrite sometimes has stronger assurance than the saint.

<u>*Why?*</u>

a) "He has not the cautious spirit, that great sense of the vast importance of a sure foundation, and that dread of being deceived. The comforts of the true saints increase awakening and caution, and a lively sense how great a thing it is to appear before an infinitely holy, just, and omniscient Judge."[139]

b) The hypocrite does not understand the depths of his spiritual blindness and the deceitfulness of his heart, as does the saint.

c) "The devil does not assault the hope of the hypocrite as he does the hope of a true saint. The devil is a great enemy to a true Christian hope," because assurance and hope encourage piety and faithfulness in the true saint, things of which Satan is greatly opposed.[140]

d) The hypocrite does not understand the depth of his depravity, as does the true saint.

The true saint, when confronted with the depth of his depravity by the light of God's awesome holiness, is both disgusted and horrified at his sinfulness, and amazed that God would save such a wretch by His mercy and grace. But "the hypocrite looks clean and bright in his own eyes."[141]

---

[136] BT, 98, footnote; Yale, 170, footnote 1.
[137] Flavel, *Touchstone of Sincerity*, in *Works* Vol. 5, 525; quoted in BT, 99; Yale, 170, footnote 1.
[138] Stoddard, *Discourse on the Way to Know Sincerity and Hypocrisy*; quoted in BT, 99; Yale, 170, footnote 1.
[139] BT, 100; Yale, 172.
[140] BT, 101; Yale, 172.
[141] BT, 101; Yale, 172-173.

3) Two types of hypocrites

   a) The *legal* hypocrite

   "Deceived with their outward morality and external religion."[142]

   b) The *evangelical* hypocrite

   "Those that are deceived with false discoveries and elevations; who often cry down works and men's own righteousness, and talk much of free grace, but at the same time make a righteousness of their discoveries and of their humiliation, and exalt themselves to heaven with them."[143]

   Note: There are many ways to be self-righteous.

   i) Basis of this false assurance

   "Impulses and supposed revelations (sometimes with Scripture, and sometimes without)...calling these impulses the witness of the Spirit."[144]

   ii) Nature of this false assurance

      a. Self-serving

      "Those that have had visions and impulses about other things, it has generally been to reveal such things as they are desirous and fond of: and no wonder that persons who give heed to such things have the same sort of visions or impressions about their own eternal salvation, to reveal to them that their sins are forgiven them, that their names are written in the book of life, that they are in high favour with God...and especially when they earnestly seek, expect, and wait for evidence of their election and salvation this way."[145]

      "And, above all things else, it is easy to be accounted for that impressions and impulses about that which is so pleasing, so suiting their self-love and pride, as their being the dear children of God, distinguished from most of the world in his favor."[146]

      b. Unshaken by sin

      "This kind of confidence of hypocrites will not be shaken by sin; they (at least some of them) will maintain their boldness in their hope, in the most corrupt frames and wicked ways; which is a sure evidence of their delusion."[147]

4) An improper view of faith leads to false assurance.

   What does it mean to "walk by faith and not by sight," to "trust God in the dark," and "trust Christ and not your experiences"?

---

[142] BT, 101; Yale, 173.
[143] BT, 101; Yale, 173.
[144] BT, 102; Yale, 173.
[145] BT, 102; Yale, 173.
[146] BT, 102; Yale, 174.
[147] BT, 103; Yale, 174.

a) Properly understood

"Scripture speaks of living or walking by faith and not by sight, in no other way than…being governed by a respect to eternal things, that are the objects of faith, and are not seen, and not by a respect to temporal things, which are seen; and believing things revealed, that we never saw with bodily eyes; and also living by faith in the promise of future things, without yet seeing or enjoying the things promised, or know the way how they can be fulfilled."[148]

John 20:29
Romans 8:24
2 Corinthians 4:7, 18
Hebrews 11:1, 8, 13, 17, 27, 29

To trust God in the dark is an exhortation to believers to trust God in the midst of difficult circumstances, when either circumstances or emotions cause us to doubt the power, goodness, faithfulness, love of God, etc. We are to hold fast to His promises, to the truth of His Word, despite anything to the contrary. It is an encouragement to *walk* in faith.

b) Improperly understood

i) Faith without life and light

"It is truly the duty of those who are thus in darkness, to come out of darkness into light and believe. But that they should confidently believe and trust, while they yet remain without spiritual light or sight, is an anti-scriptural and absurd doctrine. The Scripture is ignorant of any such faith in Christ of the operation of God, that is not founded in a spiritual sight of Christ. That believing on Christ, which accompanies a title to everlasting life, is a 'seeing the Son, and believing on him.' John 6:40. True faith in Christ is never exercised any further than persons 'behold as in a glass the glory of the Lord, and have the knowledge of the glory of God in the face of Jesus Christ,' 2 Cor. 3:18, and 4:6. They into whose minds 'the light of the glorious gospel of Christ, who is the image of God, does not shine, believe not,' 2 Cor. 4:4. That faith…without spiritual light is…presumption."[149]

"Men not only cannot exercise faith without some spiritual light, but they can exercise faith only just in such proportion as they have spiritual light. Men will trust in God no further than they know Him; and they cannot be in exercise of faith in Him one ace further than they have a sight of His fullness and faithfulness in exercise."[150]

"It is just as impossible for men to have a strong or lively trust in God when they have no lively exercises of grace…as it is for them to be in the lively exercises of grace without the exercises of grace."[151]

---

[148] BT, 103-104; Yale, 175.
[149] BT, 104; Yale, 175-176.
[150] BT, 104; Yale, 176.
[151] BT, 105; Yale, 176.

In other words, to "trust God in the dark" is *not* an exhortation to unbelievers, or even professing believers, to trust that they are saved when there is no evidence of the grace of God in their life and no light and understanding of the excellence of Christ and the gospel. To be assured of one's salvation when one has no new life and spiritual understanding of Christ is presumption. Such should be exhorted to trust in Christ, not assured that they are already saved. It is presumption to believe you are saved when there are no evidences of the grace of God in your life. If one has no evidence of the grace of God in one's life, it is probably because there is no grace of God in one's life.

ii) Improper "faith in faith," or, "I believe that I believe"

During the Awakening some misinterpreted what it means to "trust God in the dark" and taught that it was dishonoring to God to doubt one's salvation, whether or not there was evidence of God's work in one's heart and understanding. Doubters were exhorted to believe they were saved, regardless of the state of their soul.

But:

"Men do not know that they are godly by believing that they are godly. We know many things by faith, Heb. 11:3. 'By faith we understand that the worlds were made by the word of God.' Faith is the evidence of things not seen, Heb. 11:1. Thus men know the Trinity of persons of the Godhead; that Jesus Christ is the Son of God; that he that believes in Him will have eternal life; the resurrection of the dead. And if God should tell a saint that he hath grace, he might know it by believing the Word of God. But it is not this way that godly men do know that they have grace. It is not revealed in the Word, and the Spirit of God doth not testify it to particular persons."[152]

"Scripture represents faith as that by which men are brought in a good estate; and therefore it cannot be the same thing as believing that they are already in a good estate."[153]

In other words, there is no passage that specifically states that John Doe has exercised saving faith. The issue is: *If* you believe in Christ, you will be saved, but how do you know that you have truly believed? True faith does not answer "because I believe I believe," or "I have faith that I have faith." Rather, true faith answers I *know* I am saved because I have *faith* in Christ alone. The object of faith is God and Christ, not one's own faith. Put another way, one is not saved by believing he or she is saved, but by believing in Christ.

C) The relationship of love to God and sin to assurance of salvation

1) As love for God increases, assurance increases; when love for God decreases, assurance decreases.

"God contrived and constituted things...towards His own people, that when their love decays, and the exercises of it fail or become weak, fear should arise; for then they need

---

[152] Stoddard, *A Treatise Concerning the Nature of Saving Conversion*, quoted in BT, 106, footnote; Yale, 177, footnote 4.
[153] BT, 106; Yale, 178.

it to restrain them from sin, and to excite them to care for the good of their souls, and so to stir them up to watchfulness and diligence in religion. But God hath so ordered, that when love rises and is in vigorous exercise, then fear should vanish and be driven away; for then they need it not, having a higher and more excellent principle in exercise, to restrain them from sin and stir them up to their duty.....If one of these should not prevail [fear or love], as the other decays, God's people, when fallen into dead and carnal frames, when love is asleep, would be lamentably exposed indeed."[154]

Note: When Edwards speaks of fear in this context, he is speaking of a fear regarding one's secure state before God (i.e., more fear equals less assurance).

"Love is the spirit of adoption, or the childlike principle; if that slumbers, men fall under fear, which is the spirit of bondage or the servile principle; and so on the contrary. And if it be so, that love, or the spirit of adoption, be carried to a great height, it quite drives away all fear and gives full assurance; agreeable to that of the apostle, 1 John 4:8, 'There is no fear in love, but perfect love casts out fear.'"[155]

For example, the greatest motivation for children to honor and obey their parents is their parents' love for them (and thus the children's love for them), but when children take that love for granted and deliberately rebel, the rod becomes an effective incentive to obedience.

2) When sin increases, assurance decreases.

"These two opposite principles of lust and holy love bring hope and fear into the hearts of God's children in proportion as they prevail."[156]

When we sin we grieve and quench the work of the Holy Spirit in our heart. As assurance is ultimately the work of the Holy Spirit in the heart of a believer ("the Spirit Himself bears witness with our spirit that we are children of God," Romans 8:16), the more we quench the Spirit by sinning, the more we lose assurance. Additionally, God's manner is not to make His children comfortable in their sin. True love does not make loved ones comfortable in wicked and self-destructive behavior. Sin is always the enemy of assurance.

Hebrews 6:11-12: "And we desire that every one of you do shew the same diligence to the full assurance of hope unto the end: that ye be not slothful, but followers of them who through faith and patience inherit the promises."

---

[154] BT, 108; Yale, 179.
[155] BT, 108; Yale, 179-180.
[156] BT, 108; Yale, 180.

Illustrated:

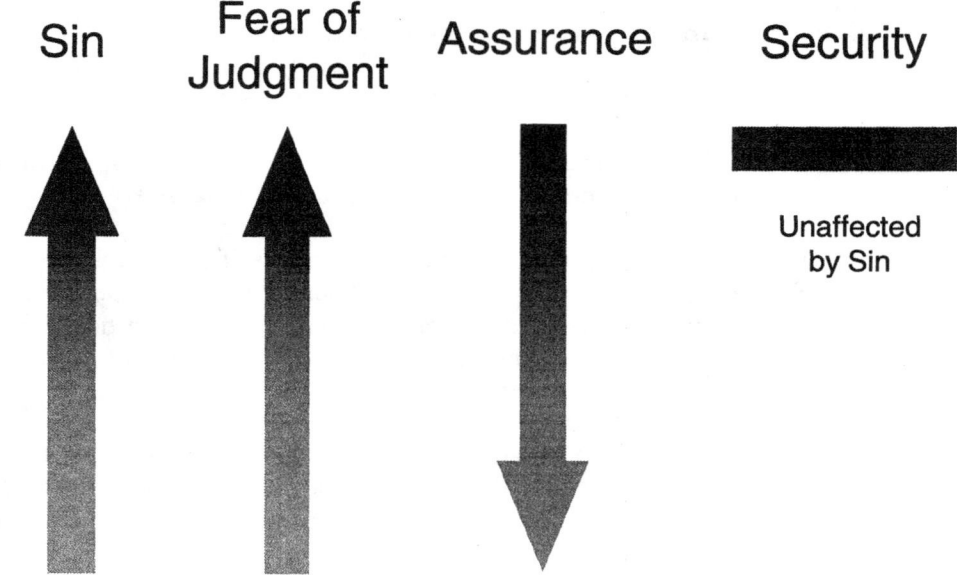

"Perfect love casts out fear, because fear involves punishment" 1 John 4:18

Note: Although the above illustration has security unaffected by sin, this is not to affirm what Edwards here denies, that people are saved regardless of the state of their soul and life. From God's perspective, the one who has truly trusted Christ is eternally secure and God only knows who are His with perfect unwavering assurance. Nonetheless, we can only know that we have truly trusted in Christ by the evidences God gives us.

3) God's design is to restrain sin in believers and false assurance in unbelievers.

"They therefore do directly thwart God's wise and gracious constitution of things, who exhort others to be confident in their hope when in dead frames; under a notion of 'living by faith, and not by sight, and trusting God in the dark, and living upon Christ, and not upon experiences;' and warn them not to doubt of their good estate, lest they should be guilty of the dreadful sin of unbelief. And it has a direct tendency to establish the most presumptuous hypocrites, and to prevent their ever calling their state in question, how much soever wickedness rages and reigns in their hearts, and prevails in their lives, under a notion of honouring God, by hoping against hope, and confidently trusting in God, when things look very dark. And, doubtless, vast has been the mischief that has been done this way."[157]

---

[157] BT, 109; Yale, 180.

Questions and Points for Discussion

1) What is the difference between assurance and security? In what way are they intimately connected?

2) How could the promises of God be of comfort to people if they could not know that those promises applied to them?

3) When people who once were assured of salvation lose assurance, does that mean they still have security or that they never had security? How can you know?

4) How would Edwards' discussion of assurance effect the way one would interpret Hebrews 3:12-4:11, 6:4-12, and 10:26-39?

5) For Edwards, is fear of judgment the highest motivation for Christian obedience?

6) Is it proper to question someone's salvation? Why or why not? When?

SESSION EIGHT

Suggested Reading:

- *The Religious Affections*, Banner of Truth, 110-119; or
- *The Religious Affections*, Yale University Press, 181-190.

Sign XII: That One's Religious Affections and Testimonies Move the Hearts of Saints

Some proponents of the Awakening were confident that the outward displays of religious affections (i.e., the eleven signs mentioned above) were sufficient to determine *with certainty* whether or not one was truly saved.

<u>But</u>:

A) "Though they know experimentally what true religion is in the internal exercises of it, yet these are what they can neither feel nor see in the heart of another."[158]

1 Samuel 16:7b: "The Lord seeth not as man seeth; for man looketh on the outward appearance, but the Lord looketh on the heart."

Note: We have seen that all of the above outward manifestations of religious affections can be either true or false, either the work of the Spirit of God, or the fruit of the deceptions of Satan and a sin darkened heart. Thus, "Men may have the knowledge of their own conversion: the knowledge that other men have of it is uncertain, because no man can look into the heart of another and see the workings of grace there."[159]

B) The *semblance* of piety "may appear in men who are altogether graceless."[160]

1) As seen by the uncertainty of the above eleven signs

2) As seen by the apostasy of "eminent saints"

"Be not offended if you see great cedars fall, stars fall from heaven, great professors die and decay: do not think they be all such: do not think that the elect shall fall. Truly, some are such that when they fall, one would think a man truly sanctified might fall away....I speak this, because the Lord is shaking; and I look for great apostasies: for God is trying all His friends, through all the Christian world. In Germany what profession was there! Who would have thought it? The Lord, who delights to manifest that openly which was hid secretly, sends a sword and they fall."[161]

---

[158] BT, 110; Yale, 181.
[159] Stoddard, *A Treatise Concerning the Nature of Saving Conversion*, quoted in BT, 110, footnote; Yale, 181, footnote 5.
[160] BT, 111; Yale, 182.
[161] Shepard, *Parable of the Ten Virgins*, 190; quoted in BT, 111, footnote; Yale, 182, footnote 7.

"It is with professors of religion, especially such as become so in a time of outpouring of the Spirit of God, as it is with blossoms in the spring; there are vast numbers of them upon the trees, which all look fair and promising; but yet many of them never come to anything."[162]

1 John 2:19

C) It is natural and proper for saints to be moved by the testimony of professing believers, regardless of whether or not the speaker's heart is right with God.

1) God's children rejoice in God's work.

"A true saint greatly delights in holiness; it is a most beautiful thing in his eyes; and God's work, in savingly renewing and making holy and happy, a poor, and before-perishing soul, appears to him a most glorious work: no wonder, therefore, that his heart is touched and greatly affected."[163]

Psalm 55:12-14

2) Error may cause godly responses.

Some held that if a believer is moved to a heart of love toward another in response to their testimony, given that the Holy Spirit is the author of Christian love, He must be the author of the response of love. As the Spirit knows who are His and is infallible and cannot lie, the person giving the testimony must therefore be a true Christian. In other words, the Holy Spirit would not be moved by a false testimony or testimony by someone who is deceived.

But:

a) We are required by God to love those whom we believe to be children of God, even if God knows otherwise. God has not made us omniscient, but has given us His Word as the infallible rule by which to judge all things.

"When there are many probable appearances of piety in others, it is the duty of the saints to receive them cordially into their charity, and to love them and rejoice in them, as their brethren in Christ Jesus."[164]

"As we ought to love Christ to the utmost capacity of our nature, so it is our duty to love those who, we think, are so near and dear to Him as His members, with an exceeding dear affection, as Christ has loved us; and therefore it is sin in us not to love them so."[165]

b) God has reserved the judgment of men's hearts to Himself.

"It is the glorious prerogative of the omniscient God, as the great Searcher of hearts, to be able well to separate between sheep and goats."[166]

---

[162] BT, 113-114; Yale, 184-185.
[163] BT, 113; Yale, 184.
[164] BT, 111; Yale, 182.
[165] BT, 116; Yale, 187-188.
[166] BT, 112; Yale, 183.

"And how arrogant must the notion be that they have, who imagine they can certainly know others' godliness, when that great Apostle Peter pretends not to say any more concerning Silvanus, than that he was a faithful brother, as he supposed! 1 Pet. 5:12: though this Silvanus appears to have been a very eminent minister of Christ, an evangelist, a famous light in God's church at that day, and an intimate companion of the apostles."[167]

1 Corinthians 4:5: "Therefore judge nothing before the time, until the Lord come, who both will bring to light the hidden things of darkness, and will make manifest the counsels of the heart: and then shall every man have praise of God."

2 Corinthians 1:19
1 Thessalonians 1:1
2 Thessalonians 1:1

    c) The Holy Spirit prompts believers to obey in all circumstances, even when He knows the catalyst is false.

Edwards illustrates the point this way: If you were told your house had burned down but that your family was unharmed, you would rightfully thank God for their safety, even if you later found out that the story was not true. To not respond with thankfulness to God at that time would have been sin.

D) God's appointed manner in judging others' sincerity is spiritual fruit.

"In the parable of the wheat and the tares it is said, Matt. 13:26, 'When the blade was sprung up, and brought forth fruit, then appeared the tares also.' As though the tares were not discerned, nor distinguishable from the wheat, until then, as Mr. Flavel observes. He mentions it as an observation of Jerome's, that 'wheat and tares are so much alike, until the blade of the wheat comes to bring forth the ear, that it is next to impossible to distinguish them.'"[168]

Questions and Points for Discussion

1) Review the 12 uncertain signs. What common characteristics render them uncertain evidences of the work of the Holy Spirit?

---

[167] BT, 118-119; Yale, 189-190.
[168] BT, 114-115; Yale, 185-186.

2) Have you ever heard a moving testimony by someone who later abandoned his or her professed faith in Christ? Have you ever known a minister of the Gospel who later denied Christ and Christianity? How might Edwards explain such apostasies?

3) When people abandon their profession of faith in Christ, what does that tell you about their original profession of faith and the source of affections that may have accompanied it, according to Edwards?

4) Why is it important to understand that the above signs are inadequate to determine whether or not religious affections are from God?

5) How was the Great Awakening affected by a lack of discernment regarding the uncertain signs?

6) Does the church today exhibit more or less discernment than the church in Edwards' day in interpreting the nature of religious affections?

PART THREE

True Signs of God's Work in the Affections of a True Believer

SESSION NINE

*Qualifications and the Fruit
of the Permanent Indwelling of the Holy Spirit*

Suggested Reading:

- *The Religious Affections*, Banner of Truth, 120-165; or
- *The Religious Affections*, Yale University Press, 193-239.

Introduction and Necessary Qualifications

A) God alone knows the heart infallibly

"I am far from undertaking to give such signs of gracious affections as shall be sufficient to enable any certainly to distinguish true affection from false in others, or to determine positively which of their neighbors are true professors and which are hypocrites. In so doing, I should be guilty of that arrogance which I have been condemning."[169]

Note: Edwards is *not* here speaking of those who do not believe the essential doctrines of Christianity, as such is clear evidence that one is not a believer.

B) The following signs are insufficient "to enable those saints certainly to discern their own good estate who are very low in grace, or are such as have much departed from God and are fallen into a dead, carnal, and unchristian frame,"[170] for the following reasons:

1) In order to lead them back to a proper relationship with Himself, God does not give comfort to those in a "dead, carnal, and unchristian frame."

2) Saints in such an ill frame are unable to discern the true signs of gracious affections because:

   a) "Grace, being very small, cannot be clearly and certainly discerned and distinguished,"[171] and,

   b) Sin dulls spiritual insight.

C) "Assurance is not to be obtained so much by *self-examination* as by *action*."[172]

"It is not God's design that men should obtain assurance in any other way than by mortifying corruption, and increasing in grace, and obtaining the lively exercises of it."[173]

2 Peter 1:5-11

---

[169] BT, 120; Yale, 193.
[170] BT, 121; Yale, 193.
[171] BT, 121; Yale, 194.
[172] BT, 123; Yale, 195.
[173] BT, 123; Yale, 195.

Sign I: Gracious Affections (Religious Affections that Are a Work of God in a True Believer) Are the Fruit of the Holy Spirit that Dwells Permanently in the Believer

A) Definition of "spiritual"

Spiritual is *not*:[174]

1) A reference to the non-material part of man versus the physical body.

2) Having its seat in the soul. Pride and self-righteousness have their seat in the soul. Paul calls these *fleshly*.

   Colossians 2:18

3) To be conversant about things immaterial. The rulers of this age, whom Paul calls natural men, were conversant with things immaterial.

   Note: Scripture identifies sorcery as a deed of the flesh (Galatians 5:19-21).

4) To be subject to common grace. The *natural* and *fleshly* man is subject to common grace.

Spiritual *is*:

1) With reference to those "sanctified by the Spirit of God," as distinguished from the "unsanctified" or "natural," those without saving and sanctifying grace. The unbeliever is a natural man, without the indwelling Holy Spirit.[175]

   Romans 7:25-8:13
   1 Corinthians 2:14-15
   Galatians 5:16-26
   Colossians 2:18
   Jude 19

2) "With relation to the Holy Ghost, or Spirit of God."[176]

3) To be born of the Holy Spirit.

4) To have the Holy Spirit dwell within you permanently, "as a principle of new nature, or as a divine supernatural spring of life and action."[177]

   John 7:38-39
   John 14:14, 16-17
   1 Corinthians 3:16
   2 Corinthians 6:16

5) To be subject to the effects of the Holy Spirit "where He exerts and communicates Himself in His own proper nature."[178]

---

[174] BT, 125-126; Yale, 198-199.
[175] BT, 124-125; Yale, 197-198.
[176] BT, 126; Yale, 198.
[177] BT, 127; Yale, 200.

"The Spirit of God so dwells in the hearts of the saints that He there, as a seed or spring of life, exerts and communicates Himself, in this His sweet and divine nature, making the soul a partaker of God's beauty and Christ's joy, so that the saint has truly fellowship with the Father, and with His Son Jesus Christ, in thus having the communion or participation of the Holy Ghost. The grace which is in the hearts of the saints is of the same nature with the divine holiness, as much as it is possible for that holiness to be which is infinitely less in degree; as the brightness that is in a diamond which the sun shines upon."[179]

"There is no work so high and excellent, for there is no work wherein God doth so much communicate Himself, and wherein the mere creature hath, in so high a sense, a participation of God; so that it is expressed in Scripture by the saints 'being made partakers of the divine nature,' 2 Pet. 1:4....Not that the saints are made partakers of the essence of God, and so are *godded* with God, and *christed* with Christ, according to the abominable and blasphemous language and notions of some heretics; but, to use the Scripture phrase, they are made partakers of God's fullness, Eph. 3:17, 13, 19, John 1:16, that is, of God's spiritual beauty and happiness, according to the measure and capacity of a creature; for so the word *fullness* signifies in Scripture language. Grace in the hearts of the saints being therefore the most glorious work of God, wherein He communicates of the goodness of His nature."[180]

John 1:16
John 3:6
John 17:13, 21, 26
Romans 8:10
2 Corinthians 6:16
Galatians 2:20
Ephesians 3:17, 18, 19
Hebrews 12:10
2 Peter 1:4
1 John 4:12, 15, 16

B) The source of spiritual affections versus that of natural affections

1) Divine versus natural

"They [unbelievers] have not the Spirit of God dwelling in them in any degree; for the apostle teaches that all who have the Spirit of God dwelling in them are His, Rom. 8:9-11....And a having anything of the Spirit is mentioned as a sure sign of being in Christ, 1 John 4:13....Being a partaker of the divine nature is spoken of as the peculiar privilege of the true saints, 2 Pet. 1:4. Ungodly men are not 'partakers of God's holiness,' Heb. 12:10."[181]

2) A new spiritual or supernatural "sense" versus natural principles

"All spiritual and gracious affections are attended with and do arise from some apprehension, idea, or sensation of mind, which is in its whole nature different, yea,

---

[178] BT, 128-129; Yale, 201.
[179] BT, 129; Yale, 201-202.
[180] BT, 130-131; Yale, 203.
[181] BT, 131; Yale, 204.

exceeding different, from all that is or can be in the mind of a natural man. The natural man discerns nothing of it...and conceives of it no more than a man without the sense of taste can conceive of the sweet taste of honey, or a man without the sense of hearing can conceive of the melody of a tune, or a man born blind can have a notion of the beauty of a rainbow."[182]

1 Corinthians 2:14: "The natural man receiveth not the things of the Spirit of God, for they are foolishness to him: neither can he know them, because they are spiritually discerned."

"This new spiritual sense is not a new faculty of understanding, but it is a new foundation laid in the nature of the soul for a new kind of exercises of the same faculty of understanding. So that new holy disposition of heart that attends this new sense is not a new faculty of will, but a foundation laid in the nature of the soul, for a new kind of exercises of the same faculty of the will."[183]

Note: The nature and operation of this new sense will be more fully explained in the remaining "distinguishing signs" to be discussed below.

C) Similarities between spiritual and natural affections

"Both spiritual love and natural love are attended with delight in the object beloved; but the sensations of delight are not the same, but entirely and exceedingly diverse. Natural men may have conceptions of many things about spiritual affections; but there is something in them which is as it were the nucleus, or kernel of them, that they have no more conception of than one born blind has of colours....The love of each has many things that appertain to it which are common; it causes both to desire and delight in the object beloved, and causes grief when it is absent, etc., but yet that idea or sensation which he who knows the taste of honey has of its excellency and sweetness, as the foundation of his love, is entirely different from anything the other has or can have; and that delight which he has in honey is wholly diverse from anything that the other can conceive of, though they both delight in their beloved objects."[184]

D) Gracious and holy affections can be counterfeited.

People can experience new and surprising religious affections that are nonetheless natural and unrelated to a new spiritual sense.

"As if a poor man that had always dwelt in a cottage and had never looked beyond the obscure village where he was born, should in a jest be taken to a magnificent city and prince's court, and there arrayed in princely robes, and set on the throne, with the crown royal on his head, peers and nobles bowing before him, and should be made to believe that he was now a glorious monarch. The ideas he would have, and the affections he would experience, would in many respects be very new, and such as he had no imagination of before; but all this is no more than extraordinarily raising and exciting natural principles, and newly exalting, varying, and compounding such sort of ideas as he has by nature; here is nothing like giving him a new sense."[185]

---

[182] BT, 135; Yale, 207-208.
[183] BT, 134; Yale, 206.
[184] BT, 136; Yale, 208-209.
[185] BT, 137; Yale, 209-210.

True Signs 63

E) The nature of "impressions," "imaginations," and "visions"

> "Hence it appears, that impressions which some have received in their imagination, or the imaginary ideas which they have of God or Christ, or heaven, or anything appertaining to religion, have nothing in them that is spiritual or of the nature of true grace. Though such things may attend what is spiritual and be mixed with it, yet in themselves they have nothing that is spiritual, nor are they any part of gracious experience."[186]

"They have had lively ideas of some external shape, and beautiful form of countenance; and this they call spiritually seeing Christ. Some have had impressed upon them ideas of a great outward light; and this they call a spiritual discovery of God's or Christ's glory. Some have had ideas of Christ's hanging on the cross, and His blood running from His wounds; and this they call a spiritual sight of Christ crucified, and the way of salvation by His blood. Some have seen Him with his arms open ready to embrace them; and this they call a discovery of the sufficiency of Christ's grace and love. Some have had lively ideas of heaven, and of Christ on His throne there, and shining ranks of saints and angels; and this they call seeing heaven opened to them"[187]

"And in like manner…they have had ideas of words, as if they were spoken to them, sometimes the words of Scripture, and sometimes other words: they have had ideas of Christ's speaking comfortable words to them. These things they have called having the inward call of Christ, hearing the voice of Christ spiritually in their hearts, having the witness of the Spirit, and the inward testimony of the love of Christ, etc."[188]

But:

1) Such things are common and natural.

   "A natural man is capable of having an idea, and a lively idea, of shapes, and colours, and sounds, when they are absent, even as capable as a regenerate man is: so there is nothing supernatural in them."[189]

   As easily as the natural man can see a tree, an animal, or block of wood in his mind, he can also see an image of Christ, a cross, blood, or any such thing. As easily as he can imagine words spoken in his mind, he can imagine comforting words of Scripture.

2) They are no better than what can be seen or heard with the natural senses.

   "The external idea a man has now of Christ hanging on the cross, and shedding His blood, is no better in itself than the external idea that the Jews His enemies had, who stood round His cross, and saw this with their bodily eyes. The imaginary idea which men have now of an external brightness and glory of God is no better than the idea the wicked congregation in the wilderness had of the external glory of the Lord at Mount Sinai, when they saw it with their bodily eyes."[190]

---

[186] BT, 138; Yale, 210.
[187] BT, 139; Yale, 211-212.
[188] BT, 140; Yale, 212.
[189] BT, 141; Yale, 213.
[190] BT, 141-142; Yale, 214.

People were not saved when they saw Christ on earth or at his crucifixion, how much less are people saved by visions of Christ in their head.

3) They are not above the power of the devil.

"It is certain that the devil can excite, and often hath excited, such ideas. They were external ideas which he excited in the dreams and visions of the false prophets of old, who were under the influence of lying spirits, that we often read of in Scripture."[191]

Deuteronomy 13:1
1 Kings 22:22
Ezekiel 13:7

4) They are little different than icons.

"The image of Christ, which men conceive in their imaginations, is not in its own nature of any superior kind to the idea the Papists conceive of Christ, by the beautiful and affecting images of Him which they see in their churches...nor are the affections they have, if built primarily on such imaginations, any better than the affections raised in ignorant people by the sight of these images."[192]

5) Even if words were brought to mind by the Holy Spirit, such is a common work of the Holy Spirit, bringing no new principle of nature.

Example: Balaam[193]

6) That the impressions come with texts of Scripture and in an immediate manner is no sign that the impressions are spiritual, or that the resulting affections are spiritual.

"Supposing these words...were suddenly brought to their minds, *Fear not, it is your Father's good pleasure to give you the kingdom.* Having confidently taken up a notion that the words were immediately spoken from heaven to them, as an immediate revelation that God was their Father and had given the kingdom to them, they are greatly affected by it, and the words seem sweet to them. 'Oh,' they say, 'they are excellent things that are contained in those words!' But the reason why the promise seems excellent to them is only because they think it is made to them immediately; all the sense they have of any glory in them is only from self-love, and from their own imagined interest in the words. Not that they had any view or sense of the holy and glorious nature of the kingdom of heaven and the spiritual glory of that God who gives it, and of His excellent grace to sinful men, in offering and giving them this kingdom of His own good pleasure."[194]

To believe something to be true because of the manner in which the information came (immediately, with texts of Scripture, light, etc.) is to trust in an experience, not God. Edwards attributes many of the problems of the Awakening to this kind of misplaced trust.

7) They cannot save. The comforting promises of God do not belong to those who have not placed their trust in Christ as Lord and Savior.

---

[191] BT, 143-144; Yale 216.
[192] BT, 142; Yale, 214.
[193] BT, 143; Yale, 215.
[194] BT, 148-149; Yale, 221.

"The first comfort of many persons, and what they call their conversion, is after this manner: after awakening and terrors, some comfortable sweet promise comes suddenly and wonderfully to their minds; and the manner of its coming makes them conclude it comes from God to them; and this is the very thing that is all the foundation of their faith, and hope, and comfort."[195]

"The Spirit of God is a Spirit of truth and not of lies: he does not bring Scriptures to men's minds, to reveal to them that they have an interest in God's favour and promises when they have none, having not yet believed....No promise of the covenant of grace belongs to any man, until he has first believed in Christ; for it is by faith alone that we become interested in Christ and the promises of the new covenant made in Him: and therefore whatever spirit applies the promises of the covenant to a person who has not first believed, as being already his, must be a lying spirit, and that faith which is first built on such an application of promises is built upon a lie. God's manner is not to bring comfortable texts of Scripture to give men assurance of his love and of future happiness, before they have had a faith of dependence."[196]

"A spiritual application of an invitation or offer of the gospel consists in giving the soul a spiritual sense or relish of the holy and divine blessings offered, and the sweet and wonderful grace of the Offerer, in making so gracious an offer, and of His holy excellency and faithfulness to fulfil what He offers, and His glorious sufficiency for it; so leading and drawing forth the heart to embrace the offer, and thus giving the man evidence of his title to the thing offered. And so a spiritual application of the promises of Scripture, for the comfort of the saints, consists in enlightening their minds to see the holy excellency and sweetness of the blessings promised, and also the holy excellency of the Promiser, and His faithfulness and sufficiency; thus drawing forth their hearts to embrace the Promiser, and the thing promised; and by this means giving the sensible actings of grace, enabling them to see their grace and their title to the promise."[197]

F) The *witness* of the Spirit

1) Background

a) Meaning of the *seal* of the Spirit

"The seal of the Spirit...alluding to the seal of princes, annexed to the instrument by which they advanced any of their subjects to some high honour and dignity or peculiar privilege in the kingdom, as a token of special favour....Nothing is more royal than the royal seal; nothing more sacred, that belongs to a prince, and more peculiarly denoting what belongs to him; it being the very end and design of it to be the most peculiar stamp and confirmation of the royal authority."[198]

2 Corinthians 1:22
Ephesians 1:13
Ephesians 4:30

---

[195] BT, 149; Yale, 221.
[196] BT, 149-150; Yale, 222.
[197] BT, 153; Yale, 225.
[198] BT, 158-159; Yale, 230-231.

"The seal of the great King of heaven and earth enstamped on the heart is something high and holy in its own nature, some excellent communication from the infinite fountain of divine beauty and glory; and not merely a making known a secret fact by revelation or suggestion; which is a sort of influence of the Spirit of God that the children of the devil have often been the subjects of.[199] The seal of the Spirit is an effect of the Spirit of God on the heart, which natural men, while such, are so far from a capacity of being the subjects of, that they can have no manner of notion or idea of it."[200]

b) Meaning of the *earnest* (pledge) of the Spirit

    i) The earnest of the Spirit is a down payment.

"Now the earnest is part of the money agreed for, given in hand, as a token of the whole to be paid in due time; a part of the promised inheritance granted now, in token of full possession of the whole hereafter."[201]

    ii) The earnest of the Spirit is a deposit of new life by the Holy Spirit indwelling the believer's heart.

"What is the earnest and beginning of glory but grace itself, especially in the more lively and clear exercises of it?...What is it that is the beginning or earnest of eternal life in the soul, but spiritual life; and what is that but grace? The inheritance that Christ has purchased for the elect is the Spirit of God; not in any extraordinary gifts, but in His vital indwelling in the heart, exerting and communicating Himself there in His own proper, holy, or divine nature; and this is the sum total of the inheritance that Christ purchased for the elect."[202]

Luke 24:49
John 14-16
Acts 1:4; 2:38-39
Galatians 3:13-14
Ephesians 1:13

"It is through the vital communications and indwellings of the Spirit that the saints have all their light, life, holiness, beauty, and joy in heaven; and it is through the vital communications and indwelling of the same Spirit that the saints have all light, life, holiness, beauty and comfort on earth; but only communicated in less measure."[203]

    iii) The earnest of the Spirit is the equivalent of the *seal* of the Spirit.

2 Corinthians 1:22
Ephesians 1:13-14

---

[199] Such as Balaam.
[200] BT, 159; Yale, 231.
[201] BT, 161; Yale, 236.
[202] BT, 162; Yale, 236.
[203] BT, 162; Yale, 236-237.

iv) The earnest of the Spirit is not direct revelation.

> "Therefore this earnest of the Spirit, and first-fruits of the Spirit, which has been shown to be the same with the seal of the Spirit, is the vital, gracious, sanctifying communication and influence of the Spirit, and not any immediate suggestion or revelation of facts by the Spirit."[204]

2) Meaning of the *witness* of the Spirit

> "What has misled many in their notion of that influence of the Spirit of God we are speaking of, is the word *witness*, its being called the witness of the Spirit. Hence, they have taken it, not to be any effect or work of the Spirit upon the heart, giving evidence from whence men may argue that they are the children of God, but an inward immediate suggestion, as though God inwardly spoke to the man, and testified to him, and told him that he was His child, by a kind of a secret voice or impression."[205]

a) Use of *witness* in the New Testament

John 5:36: "But I have greater witness than that of John: for the works which the Father hath given me to finish, the same works that I do, bear witness of me, that the Father hath sent me."

John 10:25: "The works that I do in my Father's name, they bear witness of me."

Acts 14:3: "Long time therefore abode they speaking boldly in the Lord, which gave testimony unto the word of his grace, and granted signs and wonders to be done by their hands."

Hebrews 2:4: "God also bearing them witness, both with signs and wonders, and with divers miracles, and gifts of the Holy Ghost."

"So the water and the blood are said to bear witness, 1 John 5:8, not that they spoke or asserted anything, but they were proofs and evidences. So God's works of providence, in rain and fruitful seasons, are spoken of as witnesses of God's being and goodness, *i.e.*, they are evidences of these things. And when the Scripture speaks of the seal of the Spirit, it is an expression which properly denotes, not an immediate voice or suggestion, but some work or effect of the Spirit that is left as a divine mark upon the soul, to be an evidence by which God's children might be known."[206]

b) Romans 8:14-17

i) What it says

> "The Spirit's giving us witness or evidence that we are God's children, is His dwelling in us, and leading us, as a spirit of adoption, or spirit of a child, disposing us to behave towards God as to a father....And what is that but the spirit of love?"[207]

---

[204] BT, 162-163; Yale, 237.
[205] BT, 159; Yale, 231.
[206] BT, 160; Yale, 232.
[207] BT, 163; Yale, 237.

> "The spirit of bondage works by fear for the slave fears the rod: but love cries, Abba Father; it disposes us to go to God, and behave ourselves towards God as children; and it gives us clear evidence of our union to God as His children, and so casts out fear."[208]

> "Love, the bond of union, is seen intuitively: the saint sees and feels plainly the union between his soul and God; it is so strong and lively that he cannot doubt of it. And hence he is assured that he is a child."[209]

ii) What it does *not* say

> "That which many call the witness of the Spirit is no other than an immediate suggestion and impression of the fact, otherwise secret, that they are converted, or made the children of God, so that their sins are pardoned and God has given them a title to heaven."[210]

Questions and Points for Discussion

1) Why was it necessary for Edwards to introduce the section on the twelve distinguishing signs of a true work of God with a qualification?

2) Of the twelve distinguishing signs, why does Edwards begin the list with gracious affections as the fruit of the Holy Spirit that dwells permanently in the believer? In what way is this sign foundational to the remaining eleven signs?

3) According to Edwards, can one be "spiritual" without the Holy Spirit? Why or why not?

---

[208] BT, 163-164; Yale, 238.
[209] BT, 164; Yale, 239.
[210] BT, 157; Yale, 229.

4) Some itinerant preachers and evangelists of the Awakening claimed the "witness of the Spirit" as validating their authority and actions. Does this happen today?

5) Discuss Edwards' assertion that certain religious impressions, imaginations, and visions of the mind are common, natural, and little different than icons.

Session Ten

Suggested Reading:

- *The Religious Affections*, Banner of Truth, 165-179; or
- *The Religious Affections,* Yale University Press, 240-253.

Sign II: Gracious Affections Are Founded Primarily upon the Greatness of God and His Works, Apart from Self-Interest

"Now the divine excellency and glory of God and Jesus Christ, the Word of God, the works of God, and the ways of God, etc., is the primary reason why a true saint loves these things; and not any supposed interest that he has in them, or any conceived benefit that he has received from them, or shall receive from them."[211]

As will be explained further below, this is for Edwards the *primary* foundation of gracious affections, while self-interest and gratitude for the benefits conferred by God in salvation have a "secondary and consequential influence in those affections that are truly holy and spiritual."[212]

A) The opposing argument: Self-love is the foundation of all love, including love to God.

"They argue, that whoever loves God, and so desires His glory or the enjoyment of Him, desires these things as his own happiness. The glory of God, and the beholding and enjoying His perfections are considered as things agreeable to him, tending to make him happy. He places his happiness in them, and desires them as things, which (if they were obtained) would be delightful to him, or would fill him with delight and joy, and so make him happy. And so, they say, it is from self-love, or a desire of his own happiness, that he desires God should be glorified, and desires to behold and enjoy his glorious perfections."[213]

In other words, as we do what makes us happy, and as beholding the greatness of God makes us happy, we therefore desire to behold God's glory because it makes us happy. This is merely self-love, doing that which makes us happy.

But:

How did God's perfections become pleasing in the first place? "A man must first love God, or have his heart united to Him, before he will esteem God's good his own, and before he will desire the glorifying and enjoying God as his happiness."[214]

"It is not strong arguing, that because a man has his heart united to God in love, and, as a fruit of this, desires God's glory and enjoyment as his own happiness, that therefore a desire after this happiness of his own must needs be the cause and foundation of his love. It would be just as true to argue that, because a father begat a son, therefore his son certainly begat him."[215]

---

[211] BT, 166; Yale, 240.
[212] BT, 165-166; Yale, 240.
[213] BT, 166; Yale, 240.
[214] BT, 166; Yale, 241.
[215] BT, 166-167; Yale, 241.

In other words, it is illogical to say because something is an *effect* it must therefore be a *cause*. It does not follow that because we are happy when those we love are blessed, that our desire for happiness is the cause of our love to them. We delight in the success of our spouse or children because our love to them *precedes* our taking delight in their success.

B) Edwards' support for the doctrine

1) Self-love is natural (does not require the supernatural work of the Holy Spirit).

   a) Love in response to a benefit received is natural.

   Luke 6:32: "If ye love them that love you, what thank have ye? For sinners also love those that love them."

   "The devil himself knew that that kind of respect to God which was so mercenary as to be only for benefits received or depended on…is worthless in the sight of God; otherwise he never would have made use of such a slander before God against Job, as in Job 1:9-10: 'Doth Job fear God for naught? Hast not thou made a hedge about him, and about his house,' etc."[216]

   In other words, those claiming that love to God is no more than self-love are using the same argument the Devil used in slandering Job, that people love God for what they can get from Him and no more.

   b) Gratitude is possible without true love.

   "Anger in men is an affection excited against another, or in opposition to another, for something in him that crosses self-love: gratitude is an affection one has towards another, for loving him or gratifying him, or for something in him that suits self-love. And there may be a kind of gratitude without any true or proper love: as there may be anger without any proper hatred, as in parents towards their children whom they may be angry with, and yet at the same time have a strong habitual love to them."[217]

   "Saul was once and again greatly affected, and even dissolved with gratitude towards David, for sparing his life, and yet remained an habitual enemy to him."[218]

   "We have manifest instances of it in Scripture; as in the children of Israel who sang God's praises at the Red Sea, but soon forgat God's works; and in Naaman the Syrian, who was greatly affected with the miraculous cure of his leprosy, so as to have his heart engaged thenceforward to worship the God that had healed him, and Him only, excepting when it would expose him to be ruined in his temporal interest. So was Nebuchadnezzar greatly affected with God's goodness to him, in restoring him to his reason and kingdom, after his dwelling with the beasts."[219]

2) Self-love, through natural gratitude, may produce an apparent love of God that is *not* a true spiritual love of the true God

---

[216] BT, 168; Yale, 242.
[217] BT, 169; Yale, 243.
[218] BT, 169; Yale, 244.
[219] BT, 169-170; Yale, 244. See Exodus 15, 2 Kings 5:15-18, and Daniel 4, respectively.

a) Through false notions of God

"A kind of love may arise from a false notion of God...as though He were only goodness and mercy, and not revenging justice; or as though the exercises of His goodness were necessary and not free and sovereign; or as though His goodness were dependent on what is in them, and as it were constrained by them."[220]

b) Through insensitivity to one's sin and state before God

"They have no sense of the heinousness of sin as against God, and of the infinite and terrible opposition of the holy nature of God against it. And so having formed in their minds such a God as suits them, and thinking God to be such an one as themselves, who favours and agrees with them, they may like Him very well and feel a sort of love to Him."[221]

c) Through supposed revelations of God's favor

"After awakenings and distress through fears of hell, they may suddenly get a notion, through some impression on their imagination, or immediate suggestion with or without texts of Scripture, or by some other means, that God loves them, and has forgiven their sins, and made them His children; and this is the first thing that causes their affections to flow towards God and Jesus Christ.... If the matter be strictly examined, this good opinion of God was purchased and paid for in the distinguishing and infinite benefits they imagined they received from God: and they allow God to be lovely in Himself no otherwise that that He has forgiven them, and accepted them, and loves them above most in the world, and has engaged to improve all His infinite power and wisdom in preferring, dignifying, and exalting them, and will do for them just as they would have Him."[222]

"Selfish proud man naturally calls that lovely that greatly contributes to his interest, and gratifies his ambition."[223]

"The affections of the hypocrites are very often after this manner; they are first much affected with some impression on their imagination, or some impulse which they take to be an immediate suggestion or testimony from God of His love and their happiness, and high privileges in some respect, either with or without a text of Scripture; they are mightily taken with this as a great discovery, and hence arise high affections. And when their affections are raised, then they view those high affections, and call them great and wonderful experiences; and they have a notion that God is greatly pleased with those affections; and this affects them more; and so they are affected with their affections. And thus their affections rise higher and higher, until they sometimes are perfectly swallowed up: also self-conceit and a fierce zeal rise withal; and all is built like a castle in the air, on no other foundation but imagination, self-love, and pride."[224]

---

[220] BT, 170; Yale, 244.
[221] BT, 170; Yale, 244-245.
[222] BT, 171; Yale, 245.
[223] BT, 171; Yale, 246.
[224] BT, 177-178; Yale, 252.

d) Through exhilarating experiences

"What they are principally taken and elevated with is not the glory of God, or beauty of Christ, but the beauty of their experiences. They keep thinking with themselves, What a good experience is this! What a great discovery is this! What wonderful things have I met with! And so they put their experiences in the place of Christ and His beauty and fulness. Instead of rejoicing in Christ Jesus, they rejoice in their admirable experiences; instead of feeding and feasting their souls in the view of what is without them, viz., the innate, sweet refreshing amiableness of the things exhibited in the gospel, their eyes are off from these things, or at least they view them only as it were sideways. But the object that fixes their contemplation is their experience; and they are feeding their souls, and feasting a selfish principle, with a view of their discoveries. They take more comfort in their discoveries than in Christ discovered."[225]

3) The nature of true love to God

a) A true love of God is founded upon the greatness of God apart from self-interest.

"The first foundation of a true love to God is that whereby He is in Himself lovely, or worthy to be loved, or the supreme loveliness of His nature....What chiefly makes a man or any creature lovely is his excellency; and so what chiefly renders God lovely, and must undoubtedly be the chief ground of true love, is His excellency. God's nature or divinity is infinitely excellent; yea it is infinite beauty, brightness, and glory itself. But how can that be true love of His excellent and lovely nature which is not built on the foundation of its true loveliness? How can that be true love of beauty and brightness which is not for beauty and brightness' sake?"[226]

"This infinite excellency of the divine nature, as it is in itself, is the true ground of all that is good in God in any respect; but how can a man truly and rightly love God without loving Him for that excellency in Him which is the foundation of all that is in any manner of respect good or desirable in Him?"[227]

b) Self-interest is secondary to love of God.

"The saint's affections begin with God; and self-love has a hand in these affections consequentially and secondarily only. On the contrary, false affections begin with self, and an acknowledgment of an excellency in God, and an affectedness with it, is only consequential and dependent. In the love of the true saint God is the lowest foundation; the love of the excellency of His nature is the foundation of all the affections which come afterwards, wherein self-love is concerned a handmaid: but the hypocrite lays himself at the bottom of all, as the first foundation, and lays on God as a superstructure; and even his acknowledgment of God's glory itself depends on his regard to his private interest."[228]

"The saints rejoice in their interest in God, and that Christ is theirs, and so they have great reason, but this is not the first spring of their joy. They first rejoice in God as

---

[225] BT, 177; Yale, 251-252.
[226] BT, 168; Yale, 242-243.
[227] BT, 168; Yale, 243.
[228] BT, 172; Yale, 246.

glorious and excellent in Himself, and then secondarily rejoice in the fact that so glorious a God is theirs. They first have their hearts filled with sweetness from the view of Christ's excellency, and the excellency of His grace and the beauty of the way of salvation by Him, and then they have a secondary joy in that so excellent a Saviour and such excellent grace are theirs."[229]

4) The relationship between true love and true gratitude

   a) True love is the foundation of true gratitude.

   "True gratitude or thankfulness to God for His kindness to us arises from…love to God for what He is in Himself; whereas a natural gratitude has no such antecedent foundation. The gracious stirrings of grateful affection to God, for kindness received, always are from a stock of love already in the heart."[230]

   "The saint having seen the glory of God, and his heart being overcome by it and captivated with love to Him on that account, his heart hereby becomes tender and easily affected with kindnesses received."[231]

   b) "In a gracious gratitude men are affected with the attribute of God's goodness and free grace, not only as…it affects their interest, but as a part of the glory and beauty of God's nature."[232]

   "The first foundation of the delight he has in Christ, is His own beauty; He appears in Himself the chief among ten thousand and altogether lovely. The way of salvation by Christ is a delightful way to him, for the sweet and admirable manifestations of the divine perfections in it: the holy doctrines of the gospel, by which God is exalted and man abased, holiness honoured and promoted, sin greatly disgraced and discouraged, and free and sovereign love manifested, are glorious doctrines in his eyes, and sweet to his taste, prior to any conception of his interest in these things."[233]

5) Does 1 John 4:19 teach that our love of God is from self-interest?

   "We love him, because He first loved us."

   a) In light of the preceding verses, 4:9-11, the point of 4:19 "is to magnify the love of God to us…that He loved us while we had no love to Him."[234]

   b) "That God loved us when we had no love to him, the apostle proves by this argument, that God's love to the elect is the ground of their love to Him."[235]

      i) "The saint's love to God is the fruit of God's love to them, as it is the gift of that love. God gave them a spirit of love to Him, because He loved them from eternity. And in this respect God's love to His elect is the first foundation of

---

[229] BT, 176; Yale, 250.
[230] BT, 173; Yale, 247.
[231] BT, 173; Yale, 247.
[232] BT, 174; Yale, 248.
[233] BT, 176; Yale, 250.
[234] BT, 174; Yale, 249.
[235] BT, 174-175; Yale, 249.

their love to Him, as it is the foundation of their regeneration, and the whole of their redemption."[236]

Because of His great love to us, God opened our eyes to see His glory and gave us a new heart to love Him for that glory.

ii) "The exercises and discoveries that God has made of His wonderful love to sinful men by Jesus Christ, in the work of redemption, is one of the chief manifestations which God has made of the glory of His moral perfection to both angels and men; and so is one main objective ground of the love of both to God, in a good consistence with what was said before."[237]

The beauty of the perfections of God, such as His perfect holiness, justice, mercy, love, wisdom, and others, are most clearly displayed and seen by us in viewing the person and redeeming work of Christ at the cross. So also in our conversion, we see God's perfections as they relate specifically to our sin and salvation.

iii) "God's love to a particular elect person, discovered by his conversion, is a great manifestation of God's moral perfection and glory to him, and a proper occasion of the excitation of the love of holy gratitude."[238]

6) The joy of the hypocrite compared to the joy of a true saint

"This is indeed the main difference between the joy of the hypocrite and the joy of the true saint. The former rejoices in himself; self is the first foundation of his joy: the latter rejoices in God. The hypocrite has his mind pleased and delighted, in the first place, with his own privilege, and the happiness which he supposes he has attained to or shall attain to. True saints have their minds, in the first place, inexpressibly pleased and delighted with the sweet ideas of the glorious and amiable nature of the things of God. And this is the spring of all their delights and the cream of all their pleasures: it is the joy of their joy."[239]

"When they [hypocrites] hear of the wonderful things of the gospel, of God's great love in sending His Son, of Christ's dying love to sinners, and of the great things Christ has purchased and promised to the saints, and hear these things eloquently set forth, they may hear with a great deal of pleasure, and be lifted up with what they hear; but if their joy be examined, it will be found to have no other foundation than this, that they look upon these things as theirs, all this exalts them, they love to hear of the great love of Christ, so vastly distinguishing some from others; for self-love, and even pride itself, makes them affect great distinction from others. No wonder, in this confident opinion of their own good estate, that they feel well under such doctrine, and are pleased in the highest degree in hearing how much God and Christ make of them. So that their joy is really a joy in themselves and not in God."[240]

"Having received what they call spiritual discoveries or experiences, their minds are taken up about them, admiring their own experiences. What they are principally taken

---

[236] BT, 175; Yale, 249.
[237] BT, 175; Yale, 249.
[238] BT, 175; Yale, 249.
[239] BT, 175; Yale, 249-250.
[240] BT, 176-177; Yale, 251.

and elevated with is not the glory of God, or beauty of Christ, but the beauty of their experiences."[241]

Questions and Points for Discussion

1) Do we neglect the greatest need of our souls when we fail to keep the excellence of God as the focus of our preaching and teaching? Can anything or anyone in the universe compare with the infinite glorious person of God? Is anything or anyone more worthy of our love and devotion, or more able to motivate us to greater love and devotion than the excellence of God Himself? Discuss.

2) Do we sometimes emphasize God's benefits while neglecting the excellence of God who gives them? How is this done?

3) Can unbelievers appear to love God when they merely love the benefits of God? If so, how? Give examples.

4) Is it possible for unbelievers to have false assurance of salvation based upon love of the benefits of God? Explain. In what ways can believers contribute to this false assurance?

5) During the Awakening, many made professions of faith in Christ, and many were marvelously saved and persevered in their love to Christ. Nonetheless, when the excitement and popularity of the Awakening died down, so also did the zeal of many making great professions of love to Christ during the Awakening, such that many no longer professed faith in Christ. Some interpreted this as an indication that true Christians fell away from faith in Christ. How could Edwards' distinction between a love of God for His benefits apart from a love of God for the beauty of His perfections help explain why many who were outwardly zealous for Christ fell away when the excitement of the Awakening ceased?

---

[241] BT, 177; Yale, 251.

Session Eleven

Suggested Reading:

- *The Religious Affections*, Banner of Truth, 179-192; or
- *The Religious Affections*, Yale University Press, 253-266.

Sign III: Gracious Affections Are Founded upon the "Loveliness" of the Holiness of God and His Works

"It has been already shown, under the former head, that the first objective ground of all holy affections is the supreme excellency of divine things as they are in themselves, or in their own nature. I now proceed further, and say *more particularly* that that kind of excellency of the nature of divine things, which is the first objective ground of all holy affections, is their moral excellency or their holiness"[242]

"A love to divine things for the beauty and sweetness of their moral excellency, is the first beginning and spring of all holy affections."[243]

A) *Moral* good and evil are distinguished from *natural* good and evil.

    1) *Moral* good and evil

        Moral evil is sin, i.e., that which is "against duty and contrary to what is right," while moral good is that which is in conformity with duty and what is right.[244]

        "The moral excellency of an intelligent voluntary being is more immediately seated in the heart of will."[245]

    2) *Natural* good or evil

        Natural evil is that which is contrary to nature, such as pain, suffering, and disgrace, while natural good is that which is in harmony with nature, such as pleasure, honor, and strength. Natural good and evil are both unrelated to a moral standard of right or wrong.[246]

B) "Holiness comprehends all the true moral excellency of intelligent beings."[247]

    1) Of God

        "The holiness of God in the more extensive sense of the word, and the sense in which the word is commonly, if not universally, used concerning God in Scripture, is the same

---

[242] BT, 182, emphasis mine; Yale, 256.
[243] BT, 179; Yale, 253-254.
[244] BT, 180; Yale, 254.
[245] BT, 181; Yale, 255.
[246] BT, 180; Yale 254-255.
[247] BT, 181; Yale, 255.

with the moral excellency of the divine nature, or His purity and beauty as a moral agent, comprehending all His moral perfections, His righteousness, faithfulness, and goodness. As in holy men, their charity, Christian kindness, and mercy, belong to His holiness."[248]

2) Of man

"Holiness comprehends all the true virtue of a good man, his love to God, his gracious love to men, his justice, his charity and bowels of mercies, his gracious meekness and gentleness; all other true Christian virtues that he has, belong to his holiness."[249]

C) The beauty of *natural* good in God and man is founded upon *moral* good (holiness)

1) As illustrated by angels and demons

Both possess great strength and influence (natural good), but angels are morally good, and therefore lovely, while demons are morally evil, and therefore contemptible.

Point: "Strength and knowledge do not render any beings lovely without holiness, but more hateful; though they render them more lovely when joined with holiness."[250]

2) The holiness of God is the beauty of God.

a) The *moral* and *natural* attributes of God

i) The *moral* attributes of God

"By the moral perfections of God, they [theologians] mean those attributes which God exercises as a moral agent, or whereby the heart and will of God are good, right, and infinitely becoming and lovely; such as His righteousness, truth, faithfulness, and goodness; or, in one word, His holiness."[251]

ii) The *natural* attributes of God

"Those attributes wherein, according to our way of conceiving of God, consists, not the holiness or moral goodness of God, but his greatness: such as His power, His knowledge, whereby He knows all things, and His being eternal, from everlasting to everlasting, His omnipresence, and His awful and terrible majesty."[252]

b) The *moral* and *natural* attributes of man

"There is a twofold image of God in man—His moral or spiritual image which is His holiness, that is the image of God's moral excellency (which image was lost by the fall), and God's natural image, consisting in man's reason and understanding, his natural ability, and dominion over creatures, which is the image of God's natural attribute."[253]

---

[248] BT, 181; Yale, 255-256.
[249] BT, 181; Yale, 255-256.
[250] BT, 183; Yale, 257.
[251] BT, 181; Yale, 255.
[252] BT, 181; Yale, 255.
[253] BT, 181-182; Yale, 256.

"Holiness in man is but the image of God's holiness; there are not more virtues belonging to the image than are in the Original: derived holiness has not more in it that is in that underived holiness which is its fountain."[254]

c) The beauty of all God's natural and moral attributes is God's holiness.

"Holiness is in a peculiar manner the beauty of the divine nature. Hence we often read of the beauty of holiness, Psal. 24:2, 96:9, and 110:3. This renders all His other attributes glorious and lovely. It is the glory of God's wisdom that it is a holy wisdom, and not a wicked subtlety and craftiness. This makes His majesty lovely, and not merely dreadful and horrible, that it is a holy majesty. It is the glory of God's immutability that it is a holy immutability, and not an inflexible obstinacy in wickedness."[255]

"A true love to God must begin with a delight in His holiness, and not with a delight in any other attribute; for no other attribute is truly lovely without this, and no otherwise than as…it derives its loveliness from this; and therefore it is impossible that other attributes should appear lovely, in their true loveliness, until this is seen; and it is impossible that any perfection of the divine nature should be loved with true love until this is loved."[256]

"They that do not see the glory of God's holiness cannot see anything of the true glory of His mercy and grace: they see nothing of the glory of those attributes as excellencies of God's nature, as it is in itself; though they may be affected with them and love them, as they concern their interest."[257]

3) The beauty of divine things is their holiness.[258]

a) Saints

"They are saints or holy ones; it is the moral image of God in them which is their beauty; and that is their holiness."[259]

b) Angels

"Herein consists the beauty and brightness of the angels of heaven, that they are holy angels and so not devils."[260]

Daniel 4:13, 17, 23
Matthew 25:31
Mark 8:38
Acts 10:22
Revelation 19:10

---

[254] BT, 181; Yale, 256.
[255] BT, 183; Yale, 257.
[256] BT, 183; Yale, 257-258.
[257] BT, 183; Yale, 258.
[258] BT, 184-185; Yale, 258-259.
[259] BT, 184; Yale, 258.
[260] BT, 184; Yale, 258.

c) The Word of God

Psalm 119:140: "Thy word is very pure: therefore thy servant loveth it."

Psalm 119:128: "I esteem all thy precepts concerning all things to be right; and I hate every false way."

Psalm 119:138: "My tongue shall speak of they word; for all thy commandments are righteousness."

Psalm 19:7-10

d) Christ

"He is the chief among ten thousand and altogether lovely, even in that He is the holy one of God, Acts 3:14, and God's holy child, Acts 4:27, and He that is holy, and He that is true, Rev. 3:7."[261]

"The beauty of His divine nature, of which the beauty of His human nature is the image and reflection, also primarily consists in His holiness."[262]

e) The Gospel

"It is a holy gospel, and so bright an emanation of the holy beauty of God and Jesus Christ. Herein consists the spiritual beauty of its doctrines, that they are holy doctrines or doctrines according to godliness. And herein consists the spiritual beauty of the way of salvation by Jesus Christ, that it is so holy a way."[263]

f) Heaven

"Herein chiefly consists the glory of heaven, that it is the holy city, the holy Jerusalem, the habitation of God's holiness and so of His glory."[264]

Isaiah 63:15
Revelation 21:2, 10, 11, 18, 21, 27
Revelation 22:1, 3

"It is primarily on account of this kind of excellency [holiness] that the saints love all these things."[265]

D) The true beauty of holiness is only seen and loved by true saints.

1) The true beauty of holiness is not seen and loved by the natural man.

"If persons have a great sense of the natural perfections of God, and are greatly affected with them...it is no certain sign of grace; as particularly men's having a great sense of the awful greatness and terrible majesty of God; for this is only God's natural perfection,

---

[261] BT, 184; Yale, 258.
[262] BT, 184; Yale, 259.
[263] BT, 184-185; Yale, 259.
[264] BT, 185; Yale, 259.
[265] BT, 185; Yale, 259.

and what men may see, and yet be entirely blind to the beauty of His moral perfection, and have nothing of that spiritual taste which relishes this divine sweetness."[266]

In some cases where God has revealed Himself, such as at Mt. Sinai, men "will see and know everything appertaining to his moral attributes themselves, except their beauty and amiableness; they will see and know that He is perfectly just and righteous and true and that He is a holy God, of purer eyes than to behold evil, who cannot look on iniquity. They will see the wonderful manifestations of His infinite goodness and free grace to the saints; and there is nothing will be hid from their eyes, but only the beauty of these moral attributes, and that beauty of the other attributes which arises from it."[267]

Example: Nebuchadnezzar (Daniel 4:1-3; 34-37)

The natural man may appreciate God's natural attributes and even God's moral attributes of love, mercy, and goodness, but only as they suit self-interest. He recoils from God's true holiness, loving darkness rather than the light. See John 3:19ff.

2) A holy nature loves holiness, as seen in:

   a) The new birth

   "There is given to those that are regenerated a new supernatural sense, that is as it were a certain divine spiritual taste. It is in its whole nature diverse from any former kinds of sensation of the mind, as tasting is diverse from any of the other five senses, and something is perceived by a true saint in the exercise of this new sense of mind, in spiritual and divine things, as entirely different from anything that is perceived in them by natural men."[268]

   "Various kinds of creatures show the difference of their natures very much in the different things they relish as their proper good, one delighting in that which another abhors. Such a difference is there between true saints and natural men: natural men have no sense of the goodness and excellency of holy things, at least for their holiness; they have no taste for that kind of good.... But the saints, *by the mighty power of God, have it discovered to them; they have that supernatural, most noble and divine sense given them,* by which they perceive it; and it is this that captivates their hearts, and delights them above all things."[269]

   This receipt of "that supernatural, most noble and divine sense" takes place when a person is born again, when God the Holy Spirit comes to dwell in the heart of the believer, giving the believer a new inclination (heart, will).

   b) Angels in heaven

   Isaiah 6:3
   Revelation 4:8

---

[266] BT, 189; Yale, 263.
[267] BT, 190; Yale, 264.
[268] BT, 185; Yale, 259-260.
[269] BT, 188, emphasis mine; Yale, 262.

      c) Saints in heaven

          Revelation 15:4

      d) Saints on earth

          1 Samuel 2:2
          Psalm 97:11-12
          Psalm 98:1
          Psalm 99:2, 3, 5, 8, 9

E) A heart examination

"By this, you may examine your love to God, and to Jesus Christ, and to the Word of God, and your joy in them, and also your love to the people of God, and your desires after heaven; whether they be from a supreme delight in this sort of beauty, without being primarily moved by your imagined interest in them, or expectations from them. There are many high affections, great seeming love and rapturous joys, which have nothing of this holy relish belonging to them."[270]

"The grace of God may appear lovely two ways; either as *bonum utile*, a profitable good to me, that which greatly serves my interest, and so suits my self-love; or as *bonum formosum*, a beautiful good in itself, and part of the moral and spiritual excellency of the divine nature. In this latter respect it is that the true saints have their hearts affected, and love captivated, by the free grace of God."[271]

Questions and Points for Discussion

1) Is it possible to love God but not love and desire holiness? Is it possible to love God and not see holiness as beautiful?

2) Is it proper to question the salvation of one making a profession of faith in Christ who nonetheless does not love and desire holiness? Why or why not? What is in the best interest of the one making such a profession?

---

[270] BT, 188; Yale, 262.
[271] BT, 188; Yale, 262-263.

3) If the holiness of God is that which makes God's "natural attributes" beautiful, how does this relate to our own life and testimony concerning Christ before other believers and unbelievers?

4) How do the similarities and differences between King David and Antiochus Epiphanes illustrate Edwards' understanding of the relationship between natural and moral good? (Hint: Both were kings with great power)

5) What is the relationship between God's holiness and God's justice? Can one love God's holiness and not love or appreciate the need of God's strict justice?

6) What would love without holiness look like? Is true love possible without holiness? Do we truly proclaim the excellence of God when we emphasize his love to the neglect of His holiness? Why or why not?

Session Twelve

Suggested Reading:

- *The Religious Affections*, Banner of Truth, 192-217; or
- *The Religious Affections*, Yale University Press, 266-291.

Sign IV: Gracious Affections Arise from Divine Illumination

A) The nature of divine illumination (spiritual understanding, divine enlightenment)

"Holy affections are not heat without light; but evermore arise from the information of the understanding, some spiritual instruction that the mind receives, some light or actual knowledge. The child of God is graciously affected because he sees and understands something more of divine things that he did before, more of God or Christ, and of the glorious things exhibited in the gospel; he has some clearer and better view than he had before, when he was not affected."[272]

Psalm 43:3-4
John 6:45
Romans 10:2
Philippians 1:9
Colossians 3:10
1 John 4:7

1) Divine illumination that produces gracious affections is *not*:

   a) A vision or sight of something in the imagination of the mind

   "When a person is affected with a lively idea, suddenly excited in his mind, of some shape or very beautiful pleasant form of countenance, or some shining light, or other glorious outward appearance...but there is nothing of the nature of instruction in it, persons become never the wiser by such things, or more knowing about God, or a Mediator between God and man, or the way of salvation by Christ, or anything contained in any of the doctrines of the gospel."[273]

   For example, a sudden picture or vision in the mind of Christ hanging on the cross with blood flowing from His hands, a body of great light, or any other thing that can be imagined by the mind, including sounds and voices, is not spiritual illumination.[274]

   b) A further knowledge of that which can be known by the natural man

   For example, those things revealed by the common grace of God, including the guilt of sin and the power and greatness of God.

---

[272] BT, 192; Yale, 266.
[273] BT, 193; Yale, 267.
[274] See BT, 136 or Yale, 208-209 for a description of some of the visions people had during the Great Awakening that were improperly called divine illumination.

"In those awakenings of the conscience that natural men are often subject to, the Spirit of God gives no knowledge of the true moral beauty which is in divine things; but only assists the mind to a clearer idea of the guilt of sin, or its relation to punishment, and its connection with the evil of suffering (without any sight of its true moral evil, or odiousness as sin), and a clearer idea of the natural perfections of God, wherein consists, not His holy beauty and glory, but His awful and terrible greatness."[275]

Unbelievers can see, understand, and even greatly fear God's power and justice and their desert of His condemnation, but cannot see and love the beauty of God's holiness and justice.

c) Intellectual understanding of Scripture alone

"It is possible that a man might know how to interpret all the types, parables, enigmas, and allegories in the Bible, and not have one beam of spiritual light in his mind; because he may not have the least degree of that spiritual sense of the holy beauty of divine things which has been spoken of, and may see nothing of this kind of glory in anything contained in any of these mysteries, or any other part of the Scripture."[276]

"It is plain, by what the apostle says, that a man might understand all such mysteries, and have no saving grace, 1 Cor. 13:2: 'And though I have the gift of prophecy, and understand all mysteries, and all knowledge, and have not charity, it profiteth me nothing.'"[277]

d) A manner in which Scripture comes to mind (i.e., immediately, unexpectedly, coincidentally)

"Affections arising from texts of Scripture coming to the mind are vain, when no instruction received in the understanding from those texts, or anything taught in those texts, is the ground of the affection, but the manner of their coming to the mind."[278]

e) A new interpretation or understanding of the meaning of a text of Scripture

"When the mind is enlightened spiritually and rightly to understand the Scripture, it is enabled to see that in the Scripture which before was not seen by reason of blindness. But if it was by reason of blindness, that is an evidence that the same meaning was in it before."[279]

Psalm 119:18: "Open thou mine eyes, that I may behold wondrous things out of they law."

"The office of the Spirit promised us, is not to make new and unheard-of revelations, or to coin some new kind of doctrine, by which we may be led away

---

[275] BT, 202; Yale, 276.
[276] BT, 204; Yale, 278.
[277] BT, 204; Yale, 278-279.
[278] BT, 193-194; Yale, 268.
[279] BT, 206; Yale, 280.

from the received doctrine of the gospel; but to seal and confirm to us that very doctrine which is by the gospel."[280]

   f) A Scripture text used out of context to affirm something not expressly taught in that text

   "As for instance, when persons suppose that they are expressly taught by some Scripture coming to their minds, that they *in particular* are beloved of God, or that their sins are forgiven, that God is their Father, and the like. This is a mistake or misapprehension; for the Scripture nowhere reveals the *individual persons* who are beloved, expressly; but only by consequence, by revealing the qualifications of persons that are beloved of God."[281]

   In other words, Scripture says that those who place their faith in Christ will be saved, and if you have placed your faith in Christ you are saved, but it nowhere states that John Doe in particular is saved.

2) Divine illumination that produces gracious affections *is*:

   a) Spiritual love and understanding of the beauty of the holiness of God and His works

   "Gracious affections…arise from the enlightening of the understanding to understand the things that are taught of God and Christ, in a new manner. There is a new understanding of the excellent nature of God and His wonderful perfections, some new view of Christ in His spiritual excellencies and fullness."[282]

   "Spiritual understanding…consists in 'a cordial sense of the supreme beauty and sweetness of the holiness or moral perfection of divine things, together with all that discerning and knowledge of things of religion, that depends upon and flows from such a sense.'"[283]

   2 Corinthians 4:3-4, 6

   "Spiritually to understand the Scripture is to have the eyes of the mind opened, to behold the wonderful spiritual excellency of the glorious things contained in the true meaning of it [Scripture], and that always were contained in it, ever since it was written; to behold the amiable and bright manifestations of the divine perfections, and of the excellency and sufficiency of Christ, and the excellency and suitableness of the way of salvation by Christ, and the spiritual glory of the precepts and promises of the Scripture, etc., which things are, and always were, in the Bible, and would have been seen before if it had not been for blindness, without having any new sense added, by the words being sent by God to a particular person, and spoken anew to him, with a new meaning."[284]

   Note: Divine illumination does not take place apart from God's Word. We see the beauty of the holiness of God and His works in Scripture, by the illumination of the Holy Spirit.

---

[280] Calvin, *Institutes*, 1:9:1; quoted in BT, 203, footnote; Yale, 278, footnote 2.
[281] BT, 194, emphasis mine; Yale, 268.
[282] BT, 193; Yale, 267-268.
[283] BT, 197-198; Yale, 272.
[284] BT, 206; Yale, 280-281.

b) Spiritual understanding known by saints only

"It is this kind of understanding, apprehending or discerning of divine things, that natural men have nothing of."[285]

Psalm 9:10
Matthew 11:27
John 6:40
John 14:19
John 17:3
1 Corinthians 2:14
Philippians 3:8, 10
Colossians 1:9
1 John 3:6
3 John 11

"Affections may be excited by that understanding of things which they obtain merely by human teaching, with the common improvement of the faculties of the mind. Men may be much affected by knowledge of things of religion that they obtain this way; as some philosophers have been mightily affected, and almost carried beyond themselves, by the discoveries they have made in mathematics and natural philosophy. So men may be much affected from common illuminations of the Spirit of God, in which God assists men's faculties to a greater degree of that kind of understanding of religious matters, which they have in some degree by only the ordinary exercise and improvement of their own faculties. Such illuminations may much affect the mind, as in many whom we read of in Scripture that were once enlightened.[286] But these affections are not spiritual."[287]

In other words, the Holy Spirit can and does work upon the minds of unbelievers and believers in a common way, but those influences that are "spiritual," that produce truly gracious affections, are those of the Holy Spirit while He dwells permanently in the heart of believers only. As such, "gracious affections" give evidence of a true work of the Holy Spirit in a true believer.

c) Spiritual understanding that includes the intellect and inclination (heart, will)

"Spiritual understanding consists primarily in a cordial sense, or a sense of heart, of that spiritual beauty [of God]. I say, a sense of heart; for it is not speculation merely that is concerned in this kind of understanding; nor can there be a clear distinction made between the two faculties of understanding and will as acting distinctly and separately in this matter."[288]

B) Meaning of the *leading* of the Spirit

1) The leading of the Spirit is *not* direct or indirect revelation.

"When persons have an imaginary revelation of some secret fact, it is by exciting external ideas; either of some words, implying a declaration of that fact, or some visible

---

[285] BT, 195-196; Yale, 270.
[286] An apparent allusion to Hebrews 6:4, of those enlightened by the common influences of the Holy Spirit, who nonetheless fell away, having not the permanent indwelling of the Holy Spirit.
[287] BT, 195; Yale, 269-270.
[288] BT, 198; Yale, 272.

or sensible circumstances of such a fact. So the supposed leading of the Spirit to do the will of God, is either by exciting the idea of words (which are outward things) in their minds, either the words of Scripture or other words, which they look upon as an immediate command of God....And a very great part of false religion that has been in the world, from one age to another, consists in such discoveries as these, and in the affections that flow from them."[289]

"It is chiefly by such sort of religion as this that Satan transforms himself into an angel of light: and it is that which he has ever most successfully made use of to confound hopeful and happy revivals of religion, from the beginning of the Christian church to this day."[290]

2) The leading of the Spirit defined

"It consists in two things: partly in instructing a person in his duty by the Spirit, and partly in powerfully inducing him to comply with that instruction. But so far as the gracious leading of the Spirit lies in instruction, it consists in a person's being guided by a spiritual and distinguishing taste of that which has in it true moral beauty."[291]

"A holy person is led by the Spirit, as he is instructed and led by his holy taste and disposition of heart; whereby, in the lively exercise of grace, he easily distinguishes good and evil, and knows at once what is a suitable amiable behavior towards God and towards man...and judges what is right, as it were spontaneously and of himself, without a particular deduction, by any other arguments than the beauty that is seen, and goodness that is tasted."[292]

"The children of God are led by the Spirit of God, in judging of actions themselves, and in their meditations upon, and judging of, and applying the rules of God's holy Word: and so God 'teaches them his statutes, and causes them to understand the way of His precepts.'"[293]

3) The leading of the Spirit illustrated

"If a man be a very good-natured man, his good nature will teach him better how to act benevolently amongst mankind, and will direct him on every occasion to those speeches and actions which are agreeable to rules of goodness, than the strongest reason will a man of a morose temper."[294]

"He who has a correct musical ear knows whether the sound he hears be true harmony; he does not need first to be at the trouble of the reasonings of a mathematician about the proportion of the notes. He that has a healthy palate knows what is good food as soon as he tastes it, without the reasoning of a physician about it."[295]

---

[289] BT, 212; Yale, 286.
[290] BT, 213; Yale, 287.
[291] BT, 206-207; Yale, 281.
[292] BT, 207; Yale, 282.
[293] BT, 211; Yale, 285.
[294] BT, 209; Yale, 283.
[295] BT, 207; Yale, 281.

4) A summary of Edwards' understanding of the leading of the Spirit

> To be led by the Spirit is to act according to the holy inclinations of the Holy Spirit in the transformed heart, continually enlightened and trained by the Word of God, choosing and delighting in holiness rather than the evil desires of the sinful flesh (fallen human nature).

Questions and Points for Discussion

1) Many itinerant preachers interpreted the visions and thoughts of their imagination (as noted by Edwards among the twelve uncertain signs) as the leading of the Holy Spirit. As such, the visions, and therefore the ministry of the itinerant claiming to have the visions, were said to possess the authority of God Himself. This improper understanding of the "leading of the Holy Spirit" led some to an inordinate trust in their own perceptions and opinions regarding the spiritual state of other ministers. If a minister did not preach or minister with the "proper" zeal, or if they would not allow certain itinerants into their pulpit to preach, they could be accused of being unregenerate and their congregation urged to depart the church. Many ministers and churches were greatly damaged by itinerant preachers claiming the authority of God and the "leading of the Holy Spirit" in making such accusations. Is there a lesson in this for the church today?

2) According to Edwards, does Scripture become the word of God when we understand it or have a personal experience of its transforming power, or is Scripture the objective, true, and powerful word of God as written, regardless of our understanding of it?

3) When Scripture says that unbelievers are spiritually blind, does that mean that they cannot write books that state clearly what Scripture says? If not, what is spiritual blindness, according to Edwards?

4) How does spiritual blindness and illumination relate to Edwards' understanding of the nature of the inclination (heart, will) discussed earlier?

5) The Holy Spirit is the author of Scripture, and the One who enlightens the mind and changes the inclination of the sinner. Does the Holy Spirit change the nature of the word of God when He performs his illuminating ministry? Can the word of God be properly understood as to its meaning, application, and beauty apart from the work of the Holy Spirit, according to Edwards?

6) How does Edwards' view of illumination relate to the previous three signs of a work of the Holy Spirit in a believer?

Session Thirteen

Suggested Reading:

- *The Religious Affections*, Banner of Truth, 217-237; or
- *The Religious Affections*, Yale University Press, 291-311.

Sign V: Gracious Affections Are Accompanied by the Conviction that the Gospel Is True

"The great doctrines of the gospel cease to be any longer doubtful things or matters of opinion, which, though probable, are yet disputable; but with them, they are points settled and determined, as undoubted and indisputable; so that they are not afraid to venture their all upon their truth."[296]

A) The characteristics of true belief

1) True faith includes the conviction that the things of the Gospel are true.

   Matthew 16:15-17
   John 6:68-69
   John 17:6-8
   Acts 8:37
   2 Corinthians 4:11-14, 16, 18
   2 Corinthians 5:1, 6-8
   2 Timothy 1:12
   Hebrews 3:6
   Hebrews 11:1
   1 John 4:13-16
   1 John 5:4-5

2) True belief is unique to those who are spiritual, regenerated, indwelt with the Holy Spirit.

   John 16:27
   John 17:8
   Titus 1:1
   1 John 4:15
   1 John 5:1, 10

3) True belief arises from the Holy Spirit's work of divine illumination in the heart.

4) True belief arises from a spiritual view of the beauty of the holy excellence of God and the Gospel by the Holy Spirit's work of illumination.

---

[296] BT, 217; Yale, 291.

"The mind [is] spiritually convinced of the divinity and truth of the great things of the gospel, when that conviction arises, whether directly or remotely, from such a sense or view of their divine excellency and glory as is there exhibited."[297]

"True faith arises from a spiritual sight of Christ."[298]

Matthew 16:16-17
Luke 10:21-22
John 6:40
John 17:6-8
2 Corinthians 4:3-6
Galatians 1:14-16
1 John 5:10

5) True belief is not mere mental ascent.

"If the belief of Christian doctrines be not merely from education, but indeed from reasons and arguments which are offered, it will not from thence necessarily follow that their affections are truly gracious: for in order to that, it is requisite not only that the belief which their affections arise from, should be a reasonable, but also a spiritual belief or conviction."[299]

Examples: Judas; Simon the Sorcerer (Acts 8:12, 23); the multitudes (John 2:23-25)

B) How a view of the glory and beauty of the things of the gospel convince the mind of their divinity

1) Directly

a) The glory of the Gospel is its own clear evidence.

"We cannot rationally doubt but that things that are divine, and that appertain to the Supreme Being, are vastly different from things that are human: that there is a God-like, high, and glorious excellency in them, that does so distinguish them from the things which are of men that the difference is ineffable; and therefore such as, if seen, will have a most convincing, satisfying influence upon any one that they are what they are, viz., divine."[300]

"He that is well acquainted with mankind and their works, by viewing the sun may know it is no human work. And it is reasonable to suppose, that when Christ comes at the end of the world, in the glory of His Father, it will be with such ineffable appearances of divinity as will leave no doubt to the inhabitants of the world, even the most obstinate infidels, that he who appears is a divine person. But, above all, do the manifestations of the moral and spiritual glory of the divine Being (which is the proper beauty of the divinity) bring their own evidence, and tend to assure the heart."[301]

---

[297] BT, 223; Yale, 297.
[298] BT, 223; Yale, 297.
[299] BT, 221; Yale, 295.
[300] BT, 225; Yale, 299.
[301] BT, 225-226; Yale, 299-300.

"Now this distinguishing glory of the divine Being has its brightest appearance and manifestation in the things proposed and exhibited to us in the gospel, in the doctrines there taught, the word there spoken, and the divine counsels and acts and works there revealed. These things have the clearest, most admirable, and distinguishing representations and exhibitions of the glory of God's moral perfections, that ever were made to the world."[302]

b) The evidence is seen immediately and intuitively.

"The divine glory and beauty of divine things is in itself a real evidence of their divinity, and the most direct and strong evidence. He that truly sees the divine, transcendent, supreme glory of those things which are divine, does, as it were, know their divinity intuitively."[303]

Note: For Edwards, spiritual blindness to the beauty of the things of God and the gospel in the understanding and heart prevents the unbeliever from seeing the things of God as divine and true. The work of the Holy Spirit illuminating the understanding and heart is required to see them properly and therefore as true.

"It is no argument that it cannot be seen, that some do not see it, though they may be discerning men in temporal matters. If there be such ineffable, distinguishing, evidential excellences in the gospel, it is reasonable to suppose that they are such as are not to be discerned but by the special influence and enlightenings of the Spirit of God."[304]

c) God provides sufficient and comprehensive evidence.

"The gospel of the blessed God does not go abroad a-begging for its evidence, so much as some think; it has its highest and most proper evidence in itself."[305]

"As soon as ever the eyes are opened to behold the holy beauty and amiableness that is in divine things, a multitude of most important doctrines of the gospel that depend upon it (which all appear strange and dark to natural men) are at once seen to be true."[306]

Read pages 227-228 (301-302, Yale) for an intricate and excellent discussion of how a view of the beauty of "divine things" relates to seeing the many aspects of the gospel as true.

d) Historical evidence

"But it is certain that such an assurance [of the truth of the Gospel] is not to be attained by the greater part of them who live under the gospel, by arguments fetched from ancient traditions, histories, monuments.
And if we come to fact and experience, there is not the least reason to suppose that one in a hundred of those who have been sincere Christians, and have had a heart to sell all for Christ, have come by their conviction of the truth of the gospel

---

[302] BT, 226; Yale, 300.
[303] BT, 224; Yale, 298.
[304] BT, 226-227; Yale, 300.
[305] BT, 233; Yale, 307.
[306] BT, 227; Yale, 301.

this way. If we read over the histories of the many thousands that died martyrs for Christ since the beginning of the Reformation, who have cheerfully undergone extreme tortures in a confidence of the truth of the gospel, and consider their circumstances and advantages, how few of them were there that we can reasonably suppose ever came by their assured persuasion this way; or, indeed, for whom it was possible reasonably to receive so full and strong an assurance from such arguments! Many of them were weak women and children, and the greater part of them illiterate persons, many of whom had been brought up in popish ignorance and darkness, and were but newly come out of it, and lived and died in times wherein those arguments for the truth of Christianity from antiquity and history had been but very imperfectly handled. And indeed, it is but very lately that these arguments have been set in a clear and convincing light, even by learned men themselves: and since it has been done, there never were fewer thorough believers among those who have been educated in the true religion. Infidelity never prevailed so much in any age as in this, wherein these arguments are handled to the greatest advantage."[307]

2) Indirectly

    a) "Prejudices of the heart against the truth of divine things are hereby removed [by a view of the divine glory], so that the mind thereby lies open to the force of the reasons which are offered."[308]

    "When a person has discovered to him the divine excellency of Christian doctrines, this destroys that enmity, and removes the prejudices, and sanctifies the reason, and causes it to be open and free."[309]

    For example, the miracles of Christ had a different effect upon Christ's disciples than the Pharisees.

    b) Reason is enlightened.

    "It assists and engages the attention of the mind to that kind of objects which causes it to have a clearer view of them, and more clearly to see their mutual relations. The ideas themselves, which otherwise are dim and obscure, by this means have a light case upon them, and are impressed with greater strength, so that the mind can better judge of them."[310]

C) Belief that falls short of saving belief

1) Convictions arising from "common enlightenings of the Spirit of God"

    By the common convicting work of the Holy Spirit one may have a greater perception of the natural perfections of God, such as His power and greatness, and a greater sense of one's sin and guilt before God, "and yet have no sense of the beauty and amiableness of the moral and holy excellency that is in the things of religion; and therefore no spiritual conviction of their truth."[311]

---

[307] BT, 231-232; Yale, 305.
[308] BT, 233; Yale, 307.
[309] BT, 233; Yale, 307.
[310] BT, 234; Yale, 307-308.
[311] BT 234-235; Yale, 308-309.

2) Convictions based upon false impressions or imaginations

> Such "may and often do beget a strong persuasion of the truth of invisible things. Though the general tendency of such things in their final issue is to draw men off from the Word of God, and to cause them to reject the gospel, and to establish unbelief and atheism."[312]

The object of such "counterfeit faith" is ultimately experience, not Christ alone.

3) Convictions founded upon self-interest

> "They first, by some means or other, take up a confidence that if there be a Christ and heaven, they are theirs; and this prejudices them more in favour of the truth of them. When they hear of the great and glorious things of religion, it is with this notion, that all these things belong to them. Hence they easily become confident that they are true; they look upon it to be greatly for their interest that they should be true. It is very obvious what a strong influence men's interest and inclinations have on their judgments."[313]

Questions and Points for Discussion

1) What is the difference between knowing something intuitively or immediately by sight, compared to knowing something as the deduction of a logical reasoning process? Are they mutually exclusive? Does knowing the existence and beauty of a rose by viewing it make the reality of the beauty and existence any less objectively true than if one inferred its existence and beauty through a process of logical deduction? Is the existence or beauty of the rose itself changed by someone seeing or not seeing it?

2) According to pages 227-228 (301-302, Yale), explain how the sight of the beauty of God and the things of God convinces the believer of the truth of the many aspects of the Gospel.

---

[312] BT, 235; Yale, 309.
[313] BT, 237; Yale, 310.

3) We sometimes use the expression that someone has "head knowledge but not heart knowledge." Edwards believed one could have head knowledge without heart knowledge, but heart knowledge always includes head knowledge. What did he mean by this, and how does it relate to the sign that gracious affections are accompanied by the conviction that the Gospel is true?

4) Must the truth and trustworthiness of Scripture be proven by logical and historical arguments before one can trust it as true and believe the Gospel for salvation? If not, does that make the Bible any less logically and historically true?

5) "Amazing grace, how sweat the sound that saved a wretch like me! I once was lost, but now and found, was blind, but now I see." According to Edwards, what do the blind now see?

SESSION FOURTEEN

Suggested Reading:

- *The Religious Affections*, Banner of Truth, 237-266; or
- *The Religious Affections*, Yale University Press, 311-340.

Sign VI: Gracious Affections Are Accompanied by True Humility

"Evangelical humiliation is a sense that a Christian has of his own utter insufficiency, despicableness, and odiousness, with an answerable frame of heart."[314]

A) The nature of true ("evangelical") humility in contrast to legal ("natural") humility[315]

Legal Humility	Evangelical Humility
o Natural to all people	o Peculiar to saints only
o Comes from common influences of the Holy Spirit assisting natural	o The divine work of the Holy Spirit dwelling within the saint
o May have a sense of God's natural perfections, such as His power	o Senses the moral beauty of God and divine things
o May include conviction that God will judge their sin, but with no sense of the hateful nature of sin	o Senses the vileness of self, and the hateful and vile nature of sin
o May sense one's smallness before God, but without a new nature that seeks to debase self and exalt God	o Fruit of a new heart and inclination to glorify God alone
o Conscience is active, but without spiritual understanding, a change of inclination, or submission to God.	o Includes spiritual understanding and the will inclined toward and submitted to God
o May be brought to despair of being able to help one's self	o Willingly denies and renounces self
o Subdued and forced into humility	o Brought gently to yield and delight in humility before God

---

[314] BT, 237; Yale, 311.
[315] BT, 237-239; Yale, 311-312.

B) True humility is an essential element of true religion.

"The whole frame of the gospel, and every thing appertaining to the new covenant, and all God's dispensations towards fallen man, are calculated to bring to pass this effect in the hearts of men."[316]

Psalm 34:18: "The Lord is nigh unto them that are of a broken heart, and saveth such as be of a contrite spirit."

Psalm 51:17: "The sacrifices of God are a broken spirit: a broken and a contrite heart, O God, Thou wilt not despise."

Psalm 138:6: "Though the Lord be high, yet hath he respect unto the lowly."

Proverbs 3:34: "He giveth grace unto the lowly."

Isaiah 57:15: "Thus saith the high and lofty One that inhabiteth eternity, whose name is holy; I dwell in the high and holy place, with him also that is of a contrite and humble spirit, to revive the spirit of the humble, and to revive the heart of the contrite ones."

Habakkuk 2:4: "Behold, his soul which is lifted up is not upright in him: but the just shall live by his faith."

Isaiah 66:1-2
Ezekiel 36: 26, 27, 31
Micah 6:8
Matthew 5:3
Matthew 18:3-4
Mark 10:15
Luke 7:37ff.
Luke 18:9-14
Colossians 3:12

C) Humility is the principle aspect of the Christian duty of self-denial.

1) True self-denial

a) "A man's denying his worldly inclinations, and in forsaking and renouncing all worldly objects and enjoyments" *and*

b) A "denying his natural self-exaltation, and renouncing his own dignity and glory, and in being emptied of himself"[317]

2) False self-denial

"It is inexpressible, and almost inconceivable, how strong a self-righteous, self-exalting disposition is naturally in man; and what he will not do and suffer to feed and gratify it: and what lengths have been gone in a seeming self-denial in other respects."[318]

---

[316] BT, 239; Yale, 312.
[317] BT, 241; Yale, 315.

"Many anchorites and recluses have abandoned (though without any true mortification) the wealth and pleasures and common enjoyments of the world, who were far from renouncing their own dignity and righteousness. They never denied themselves for Christ, but only sold one lust to feed another."[319]

"There are many that are full of expressions of their own vileness, who yet expect to be looked upon as eminent and bright saints by others, as their due; and it is dangerous for any so much as to hint the contrary, or to carry it towards them any otherwise that as if we looked upon them as some of the chief of Christians."[320]

"And some who think themselves quite emptied of themselves, and are confident that they are abased in the dust, are full as they can hold with the glory of their own humility, and lifted up to heaven with a high opinion of their own abasement."[321]

D) The nature of religious pride

1) The proud man thinks highly of his religious attainments and experiences as compared to others.

   a) Religious pride considered by itself

   "It is natural for him to fall into that thought of himself that he is an eminent saint, that he is very high amongst the saints, and has distinguishingly good and great experiences. That is the secret language of his heart: Luke 18:11, 'God, I thank thee that I am not as other men.' and Isa. 65:5, 'I am holier than thou.'"[322]

   "There are some persons that naturally think highly of their experiences.... This may be spoken and meant in a good sense. In one sense, every degree of saving mercy is a great thing. It is indeed a thing great, yea, infinitely great, for God to bestow the least crumb of children's bread on such dogs as we are in ourselves; and the more humble a person is that hopes that God has bestowed such mercy on him, the more apt will he be to call it a great thing....But if, by great things which they have experienced they mean comparatively great spiritual experiences, or great compared with others' experiences, or beyond what is ordinary...is the very same thing as to say, I am an eminent saint, and have more grace than ordinary."[323]

   Note: This may be the case, even though credit is given to the grace of God, as in Luke 18:11, "God, *I thank thee* that I am not as other men" [emphasis mine].

   "I do not believe there is an eminent saint in the world that is a high professor [i.e., a big talker concerning his religious attainments or experiences]. Such will be much more likely to profess themselves to be least of all saints, and to think that every saint's attainments and experiences are higher than his."[324]

---

[318] BT, 241; Yale, 315.
[319] BT, 241; Yale, 315.
[320] BT, 243; Yale, 317.
[321] BT, 245; Yale, 319.
[322] BT, 246; Yale, 320.
[323] BT, 247; Yale, 321.
[324] BT, 248; Yale, 322.

b) Religious pride considered in contrast to true humility

> "Such is the nature of grace and of true spiritual light that they naturally dispose the saints in the present state to look upon their grace and goodness little, and their deformity great."[325]

Why?

i) The greater our view of God and His grace, the smaller will appear our attainments and experiences.

> "But that is the nature of true grace and spiritual light, that it opens to a person's view the infinite reason there is that he should be holy in a high degree. And the more grace he has, and the more this is opened to view, the greater the sense he has of the infinite excellency and glory of the divine Being, and of the infinite dignity of the person of Christ, and the boundless length and breadth and depth and height of the love of Christ to sinners. And as grace increases, the field opens more and more to a distant view, until the soul is swallowed up with the vastness of the object, and the person is astonished to think how much it becomes him to love this God and this glorious Redeemer that has so loved man, and how little he does love."[326]

ii) The greater our view of God and His grace, the greater will appear our sin.

   a. The greater our view of God's infinite holiness, the greater will be our view of how far we fall short.

   > Given what God has displayed to us "of his infinite glory, in His Word, and in His works; and particularly in the gospel of His Son, what He has done for sinful man by Him" and our God-given ability to understand these reasons why we should love Him, "How small indeed is the love of the most eminent saint on earth, in comparison of what these things jointly considered do require!"[327]

   > "It appears exceedingly abominable to them that Christ should be loved so little, and thanked so little for His dying love. It is in their eyes hateful ingratitude."[328]

   b. The greater our view of God's holiness, the more vile will appear our smallest sin.

   > "It not only tends to convince them that their corruption is much greater than their goodness, which is indeed the case; but it also tends to cause the deformity that there is in the least sin, or the least degree of corruption, to appear so great as vastly to outweigh all the beauty there is in their greatest holiness."[329]

---

[325] BT, 249; Yale, 323.
[326] BT, 249-250; Yale, 324.
[327] BT, 251; Yale, 325.
[328] BT, 251-252; Yale, 325-326.
[329] BT, 252; Yale, 326.

"We are surely under greater obligation to love a more lovely being, than a less lovely; and if a Being be infinitely lovely or worthy to be loved by us, then our obligations to love Him are infinitely great; and therefore, whatever is contrary to this love, has in it infinite iniquity, deformity, and unworthiness."[330]

<u>Note</u>: To illustrate this point, consider the difference between insulting a peer versus insulting a sovereign king. The greater the excellence of the one insulted, the greater the evil of the insult.

c) Religious pride considered in contrast to true spiritual knowledge

i) "All true spiritual knowledge is such that, the more a person has of it, the more is he sensible of his own ignorance."[331]

Proverbs 26:12: "Seest thou a man wise in his own conceit? there is more hope for a fool than of him."

Isaiah 5:21: "Woe unto them that are wise in their own eyes, and prudent in their own sight!"

1 Corinthians 8:2: "He that thinketh he knoweth anything, he knoweth nothing yet as he ought to know."

Proverbs 3:7
Proverbs 30:2-4
Romans 12:16

ii) "Spiritual knowledge" that hides personal sinfulness is false.

"It is darkness that hides men's pollution and deformity; but light let into the heart discovers it, searches it out in its secret corners, and makes it plainly to appear; especially that penetrating, all-searching light of God's holiness and glory."[332]

2) The proud man thinks highly of his own humility.

A slave thinks nothing of untying the shoe of a prince, but we think our lowering our self to untie the shoe of a peer to be an act of great humility. Thus our view of our humility depends upon our view of our status in relation to those we serve. The higher we view our self and the lower we view the one we serve, the greater we will view the humility of our service.[333]

"When he says in his heart, 'This is a great act of humiliation; it is certainly a sign of great humility in me that I should feel thus and do so,' his meaning is, 'This is great humility for me, for such an one as I that am so considerable and worthy.' He considers how low he is now brought, and compares this with the height of dignity on which he in

---

[330] BT, 252; Yale, 326.
[331] BT, 256; Yale, 330.
[332] BT, 253; Yale, 327.
[333] BT, 258; Yale, 332.

his heart thinks he properly stands, and the distance appears very great, and he calls it all mere humility, and as such admires it."[334]

"Counterfeit humility is forward to put itself forth to view. Those that have it are apt to be much in speaking of their humiliations, setting them forth in high terms, and making a great outward show of humility in affected looks, gestures, manner of speech, meanness of apparel, or some affected singularity."[335]

Proverbs 30:32
Isaiah 58:5
Zechariah 13:4
Matthew 6:16-17
Colossians 2:23

"He that is truly and eminently humble never thinks his humility great. The cause why he should be abased appears so great, and the abasement of the frame of his heart so greatly short of it, that he takes much more notice of his pride than his humility."[336]

3) God hates pride and desires humility in people.

Psalm 28:27
Psalm 101:5
Proverbs 6:16, 17
Proverbs 21:4
Isaiah 65:5
Ezekiel 16:56
Romans 13:7
1 Corinthians 13:4-5
Ephesians 6:5
1 Timothy 2:9
1 Peter 2:18
1 Peter 3:15

Questions and Points for Discussion

1) Some itinerant preachers, along with other vigorous supporters of the Awakening, were unresponsive to suggestions and antagonistic to criticisms of their theology and practice, even though they were often hurting the Awakening and the correction was intended to help the cause of Christ in support of the Awakening. What factors may have contributed to their inability to receive correction?

---

[334] BT, 259; Yale, 332-333.
[335] BT, 261-262; Yale, 335.
[336] BT, 260; Yale, 333.

2) Edwards understood that ostentatious displays of humility could be no more than religious pride and hypocrisy. Given the difficulty of knowing another's heart, how can you know that someone's display of Christian humility is actually no more than natural and unsanctified self-exaltation?

3) In what ways can we be puffed up with our own "religious attainments"? What is the cure for this kind of pride?

4) Is it easy in our own hearts to tell the difference between self-pity when we suffer negative consequences of a sin versus true contrition and humility before God because we have offended Him? What are some examples of self-pity for suffering negative consequences for sin that often appear as godly humility and repentance?

5) What does an exaggerated view of one's self and attainments indicate concerning one's view of the excellence and greatness of God and His grace?

Session Fifteen

Suggested Reading:

- *The Religious Affections*, Banner of Truth, 266-285; or
- *The Religious Affections,* Yale University Press, 340-357.

Sign VII: Gracious Affections Accompany a Change of Nature

A) God alone can change the nature of the soul.

"Such power...is peculiar to the Spirit of the Lord: other power may make an alteration in men's present frames and feelings: but it is the power of a Creator only that can change the nature, or give a new nature."[337]

B) God does change the nature of the soul.

"Scripture representations of conversion do strongly imply and signify a change of nature: such as 'being born again; becoming new creatures; rising from the dead; being renewed in the spirit of the mind, dying to sin, and living to righteousness; putting off the old man, and putting on the new man; a being ingrafted into a new stock; a having a divine seed implanted in the heart; a being made partakers of the divine nature,' etc."[338]

C) In salvation, God changes the inclination of the heart from sin to God.

"Conversion is a great and universal change of the man, turning him from sin to God. A man may be restrained from sin, before he is converted; but when he is converted, he is not only restrained from sin, his very heart and nature is turned from it unto holiness: so that thenceforward he becomes a holy person, and an enemy to sin."[339]

D) The change of nature is permanent.

"If there be a very great alteration visible in a person for a while, if it be not abiding, but he afterwards returns, in a stated manner, to be much as he used to be; it appears to be no change of nature, for nature is an abiding thing. A swine that is of a filthy nature may be washed, but the swinish nature remains; and a dove that is of a cleanly nature may be defiled, but its cleanly nature remains."[340]

E) The change of nature does not imply perfection in this life.

"Conversion does not entirely root out the natural temper; those sins which a man by his natural constitution was most inclined to before his conversion, he may be most apt to fall into still. Yet conversion will make a great alteration even with respect to these sins.

---

[337] BT, 267; Yale, 340.
[338] BT, 267; Yale, 340.
[339] BT, 267; Yale, 340-341.
[340] BT, 268; Yale, 341.

Though grace, while imperfect, does not root out an evil natural temper, yet it is of great power and efficacy with respect to it, to correct it."[341]

F) Life transformation continues until perfection in heaven.

    John 4:14
    John 7:38-39
    Romans 12:1-2
    2 Corinthians 3:18

Sign VIII: Gracious Affections Promote and Are Attended with a Christ-Like Demeanor

"In other words, they naturally beget and promote such a spirit of love, meekness, quietness, forgiveness and mercy, as appeared in Christ."[342]

A) Support for the doctrine

    1) The general testimony of Scripture[343]

        Proverbs 17:27
        Matthew 5:5-9
        Luke 9:55
        1 Corinthians 13:4-5
        Galatians 5:22-23
        Colossians 3:12-13
        James 3:14-17

    2) Love, meekness, quietness, forgiveness, and mercy characterized the person and redemptive work of Jesus Christ.[344]

        Matthew 11:29
        Matthew 21:5

    3) The purpose of God is to conform us to the character of Jesus Christ.

        Romans 8:29
        1 Corinthians 15:47-49
        2 Corinthians 3:18
        Colossians 3:10

    4) Christians reflect the character of Christ.

        "Christians who shine by reflecting the light of the Sun of Righteousness shine with the same sort of brightness, the same mild, sweet, and pleasant beams."[345]

---

[341] BT, 268; Yale, 341.
[342] BT, 272; Yale, 344-345.
[343] BT, 272-273; Yale, 345-346.
[344] BT, 273-274; Yale, 346-347.
[345] BT, 274; Yale, 347.

"A Christian spirit is Christ's mark that he sets upon the souls of his people; His seal in their foreheads, bearing his image and superscription."[346]

"And in this respect the church is clothed with the sun, not only by being clothed with His imputed righteousness, but also by being adorned with his graces, Rom. 13:14."[347]

5) Christians possess the Spirit of meekness.

"The Spirit that descended on Christ when he was anointed of the Father, descended on him like a dove. The dove is a noted emblem of meekness, harmlessness, peace and love. But the same Spirit that descended on the Head of the church descends to the members."[348]

John 20:22
Romans 8:9
1 Corinthians 6:17
Galatians 4:6
Ephesians 4:4
1 John 2:20, 27

6) The terms *meek* and *godly* are used as synonyms.[349]

Psalm 37:10-11
Psalm 147:6

7) That Christ calls His followers children implies the necessity of meekness.

Matthew 10:42
Matthew 18:3, 6, 10, 14
Matthew 19:14
Mark 10:15
John 13:33
1 Corinthians 14:20

B) Two possible objections to the doctrine

1) Christians are in spiritual warfare and are to be *strong* and *bold* for Christ. True.

<u>But</u>:

a) Our understanding of Christian strength and boldness is often mistaken.

"Many persons seem to be quite mistaken concerning the nature of Christian fortitude. It is an exceeding diverse thing from a brutal fierceness, or the boldness of beasts of prey. True Christian fortitude consists in strength of mind, through grace, exerted in two things; in ruling and suppressing the evil and unruly passions and affections of the mind; and in steadfastly and freely exerting and following good

---

[346] BT, 274; Yale, 347.
[347] BT, 275; Yale, 347.
[348] BT, 275; Yale, 348.
[349] BT, 276; Yale, 349.

affections and dispositions, without being hindered by sinful fear or the opposition of enemies."[350]

"The passions that are restrained and kept under, in the exercise of this Christian strength and fortitude, are those very passions that are vigorously and violently exerted in a false boldness for Christ."[351]

"The strength of the good soldier of Jesus Christ appears in nothing more than in steadfastly maintaining the holy calm, meekness, sweetness, and benevolence of his mind, amidst all the storms, injuries, strange behaviour, and surprising acts and events of this evil and unreasonable world."[352]

b) We are to follow Christ's example.

"Behold Jesus Christ in the time of His last sufferings, when his enemies in earth and hell made their most violent attack upon Him, compassing him round on every side like rending and roaring lions....But how did He show His holy boldness and valour at that time? Not in the exercise of any fiery passions; not in fierce and violent speeches, vehemently declaiming against the intolerable wickedness of opposers, giving them their own in plain terms: but in not opening His mouth when afflicted and oppressed, in going as a lamb to the slaughter, and, as a sheep before his shearers is dumb, not opening his mouth; praying that the Father would forgive His cruel enemies because they knew not what they did; not shedding others' blood, but with all-conquering patience and love shedding His own."[353]

c) Some "boldness" is nothing more than pride.

"There is a pretended boldness for Christ that arises from no better principle than pride. A man may be forward to expose himself to the dislike of the world, and even to provoke their displeasure, out of pride. For it is the nature of spiritual pride to cause men to seek distinction and singularity; and so oftentimes to set themselves at war with those that they call carnal, that they may be more highly exalted among their party."[354]

"Hence men forsake their friends, and trample under foot the scorns of the world: they have credit elsewhere. To maintain their interest in the love of godly men, they will suffer much."[355]

"He is bold for Christ that has Christian fortitude enough to confess his fault openly, when he has committed one that requires it, and as it were to come down upon his knees before opposers. Such things as these are vastly greater evidence of holy boldness than resolutely and fiercely confronting opposers."[356]

---

[350] BT, 277; Yale, 350.
[351] BT, 277-278; Yale, 350.
[352] BT, 278; Yale, 350.
[353] BT, 278-279; Yale, 351.
[354] BT, 279; Yale, 352.
[355] Shepard, *Parable of the Ten Virgins*, 285, quoted in BT, 280, footnote; Yale, 352, footnote 7.
[356] BT, 280; Yale, 352.

2) Christians are to have great zeal for Christ.

But:

"It is indeed a flame, but a sweet one....For the flame of which it is the heat is no other than that of divine love or Christian charity, which is the sweetest and most benevolent thing that is, or can be, in the heart of man or angel."[357]

"There is nothing in a true Christian zeal that is contrary to that spirit of meekness, gentleness, and love, that spirit of a little child, a lamb and dove, that has been spoken of; but is entirely agreeable to it, and tends to promote it."[358]

C) Forgiveness, love, and mercy belong to the character of every Christian.

1) Forgiveness

Matthew 6:12, 14-15
Matthew 18:22-35
Mark 11:25-26

2) Love

John 13:34-35
John 14:21
John 15:12, 17
1 John 2:9-10
1 John 3:14, 18-19, 23-24
1 John 4:7-8, 12-13, 16, 20

3) Mercy

Psalm 37:21, 26
Psalm 112:5, 9
Proverbs 14:31
Proverbs 21:26
Jeremiah 22:16
Hosea 6:6
Matthew 5:7
2 Corinthians 8:8
James 1:27
James 2:13-16
1 John 3:17

D) Implication with respect to assurance

"Ministers, and others, have no warrant from Christ to encourage persons that are of a contrary character and behaviour to think they are converted, because they tell a fair story of illuminations and discoveries. In so doing, they would set up their own wisdom against Christ's, and judge against that rule by which Christ has declared all men should know his disciples."[359]

---

[357] BT, 280; Yale, 352.
[358] BT, 280; Yale, 353.
[359] BT, 284; Yale, 356.

Questions and Points for Discussion

1) For Edwards, Christian gentleness and meekness are compatible with Christian zeal and boldness. How are these compatible?

2) Are Christian boldness and zeal contrary to the fruits of the Holy Spirit?

3) Which of the following scenarios better represents Christian boldness to Edwards: 1) an itinerant preacher willing to get into the face of his hearers and preach Christ day or night at the top of his lungs in the market square and in his own pulpit, and a willingness to interrupt a worship service and call the preacher unregenerate, to the approval of his followers; or 2) someone sharing his or her faith with unbelievers, with sweetness, humility, and gentleness, in the face of possible opposition and scorn?

4) The seeking of one's own significance and distinction from others is a characteristic of our modern culture, but Edwards saw it as a form of pride. Is he correct? Why or why not?

5) What does it mean to vigorously contend for the faith, but with the demeanor of Christ?

SESSION SIXTEEN

Suggested Reading:

- *The Religious Affections*, Banner of Truth, 285-308; or
- *The Religious Affections*, Yale University Press, 357-383.

Sign IX: Gracious Affections "Soften the Heart"

A) The effects of false affections

1) False affections ultimately harden the heart.

   "With the delusion that attends them, they finally tend to stupefy the mind and shut it up against those affections wherein tenderness of heart consists: and the effect of them at last is that persons become less affected with their present and past sins, and less conscientious with respect to future sins, less moved with the warnings and cautions of God's word or God's chastisements in His providence, more careless of the frame of their hearts and the manner and tendency of their behaviour, less quick-sighted to discern what is sinful, less afraid of the appearance of evil, than they were while they were under legal awakenings and fears of hell."[360]

2) False affections ultimately lead to license.

   "They trust Christ to preserve to them the quiet enjoyment of their sins, and to be their shield to defend them from God's displeasure; while they come close to Him, even to His bosom, the place of His children, to fight against Him, with their mortal weapons hid under their skirts. However, some of these at the same time make a great profession of love to God, and assurance of His favour, and great joy in tasting the sweetness of His love."[361]

   Jude 4

B) The effects of gracious affections

1) They soften the heart toward God, His commands, and others.

   Illustration: The nature of children

   A summary here of Edwards' marvelous discussion comparing the nature of a child to the "tenderness of the heart of a true Christian" would not do it justice. Take time to read the paragraph, beginning at the third paragraph, respectively, of page 287 (BT) and page 360 (Yale).

---

[360] BT, 285; Yale, 358.
[361] BT, 286-287; Yale, 359.

2) They heighten the conscience.

"Grace does not stupefy a man's conscience, but makes it more able thoroughly to discern the sinfulness of that which is sinful, and to receive a greater conviction of the heinous and dreadful nature of sin."[362]

3) They stimulate Christian joy and hope.[363]

C) Answering a possible objection: What about holy boldness in prayer and worship?

Answer: Holy boldness is not contrary to reverence and humility.

"Gracious affections do not tend to make men bold, forward, noisy, and boisterous; but rather to speak trembling....It tends to clothe them with a kind of holy fear in all their behaviour towards God and man."[364]

Psalm 2:11
Romans 11:20
2 Corinthians 7:15
Ephesians 6:5
1 Peter 3:2, 15

"Holy boldness is not in the least opposite to reverence; though it be to disunion and servility. It abolishes or lessens that disposition which arises from moral distance or alienation; and also distance of relation, as that of a slave; but not at all that which becomes the natural distance, whereby we are infinitely inferior. No boldness in poor sinful worms of the dust, that have a right sight of God and themselves, will prompt them to approach to God with less fear and reverence than spotless and glorious angels in heaven, who cover their faces before his throne."[365]

"There is in some persons a most unsuitable and insufferable boldness, in their addresses to the great Jehovah, in an affectation of a holy boldness, and ostentation of eminent nearness and familiarity; the very thoughts of which would make them shrink into nothing, with horror and confusion, if they saw the distance that is between God and them. They are like the Pharisee, that boldly came up near in a confidence of his own eminency in holiness."[366]

Note: Edwards has in mind here some of the loud, ostentatious, and proud itinerant preachers of the Great Awakening. He is *not* denying that true saints can freely approach God with the loving familiarity of a child to a father.

Sign X: Gracious Affections Have a Beautiful Symmetry and Balance

A) Qualification

"Not that the symmetry of the virtues, and gracious affections of the saints is perfect in this life: it oftentimes is in many things defective, through imperfection of grace, lack of proper

---

[362] BT, 290; Yale, 363.
[363] BT, 293; Yale, 364.
[364] BT, 288; Yale, 361.
[365] BT, 289; Yale, 361-362.
[366] BT, 289-290; Yale, 362.

instructions, errors in judgment, some particular unhappiness of natural temper, defects in education, and many other disadvantages that might be mentioned. But yet there is in no wise that monstrous disproportion in gracious affections, and the various parts of true religion in the saints, that is very commonly to be observed in the false religion and counterfeit graces of hypocrites."[367]

B) The reason for the symmetry of gracious affections: the universal nature of sanctification.

  1) Believers are recreated in the whole image of Christ.

     "They have the whole image of Christ upon them: they have put off the old man, and have put on the new man entire in all his parts and members. It hath pleased the Father that in Christ all fullness should dwell: there is in Him every grace; He is full of grace and truth: and they that are Christ's 'of his fullness receive, and grace for grace.'"[368]

  2) There is a symmetry and beauty in all of God's workmanship.

     "The natural body, which God hath made, consists of many members; and all are in a beautiful proportion. So it is in the new man, consisting of various graces and affections."[369]

C) The nature of the symmetry and beauty of gracious affections

  1) Gracious affections are balanced and appropriate in their *kind*:

     "In some hypocrites is the most confident hope, while they are void of reverence, self-jealousy and caution, and while they to a great degree cast off fear. In the saints, joy and holy fear go together, though the joy be never so great: as it was with the disciples, in that joyful morning of Christ's resurrection, Matt. 28:8: 'and they departed quickly from the sepulcher, with fear and great joy.'"[370]

     "The joy and comfort of the [saint] is attended with godly sorrow and mourning for sin."[371]

     Matthew 5:4: "Blessed are they that mourn; for they shall be comforted."

  2) Gracious affections are balanced and appropriate in their *objects*:

     a) Toward *God* and *people*

        "Some make high pretenses and a great show of love to God and Christ...but they have not a spirit of love and benevolence towards men."[372]

        1 John 4:20

---

[367] BT, 292; Yale, 365.
[368] BT, 292; Yale, 364.
[369] BT, 292-293; Yale, 365.
[370] BT, 293; Yale, 366.
[371] BT, 293; Yale, 366.
[372] BT, 294; Yale, 367-368.

b) Toward *friends* and *adversaries*

> Some "are knit to their own party, them that approve of them, love them and admire them; but are fierce against those that oppose and dislike them."[373]

Matthew 5:45-46

c) Toward those *far* and *near*

> "Some show a great affection to their neighbours, and pretend to be ravished with the company of the children of God abroad; but at the same time are uncomfortable and churlish towards their wives and other near relations at home, and are very negligent of relative duties."[374]

d) Concerning the *physical* and *spiritual* needs of people

> "Some men show a love to others as to their outward man; they are liberal of their worldly substance, and often give to the poor, but have no love to, or concern for, the souls of men. Others pretend a great love to men's souls that are not compassionate and charitable towards their bodies. To make a great show of love, pity, and distress for souls, costs them nothing."[375]

Christ ministered to both.

e) Toward *others* and *ourselves*

> "It is a sign that affections are not of the right sort, if persons seem to be much affected with the bad qualities of their fellow Christians, as the coldness and lifelessness of other saints, but are in no proportion affected with their own defects and corruptions."[376]

f) Concerning religious "attainments"

> "If persons pretend that they come to high attainments in religion, but have never yet arrived to the lesser attainments, it is a sign of a vain pretense."[377]

> "If they pretend to be brought to be even willing to be damned for the glory of God, but have no forwardness to suffer a little in their estates and names and worldly convenience, for the sake of their duty...their pretenses are manifestly vain."[378]

g) Concerning proper religious priorities

> "So it is with religious desires and longings: these in the saints, are to those things that are spiritual and excellent in general, and that in some proportion to their excellency, importance or necessity...but in false longing it is often far otherwise. They will

---

[373] BT, 294; Yale, 368.
[374] BT, 295; Yale, 368.
[375] BT, 295; Yale, 369.
[376] BT, 296; Yale, 369-370.
[377] BT, 296; Yale, 370.
[378] BT, 297; Yale, 370.

strangely run, with an impatient vehemence, after something of less importance, when other things of greater importance are neglected."[379]

"Some persons from time to time are attended with a vehement inclination, and unaccountably violent pressure, to declare to others what they experience, and to exhort others; when there is at the same time no inclination, in any measure equal to it, to other things, to which true Christianity has a great, yea, a greater tendency; as the pouring out of the soul before God in secret, earnest prayer and praise to Him, and for more conformity to Him, and living more to His glory, etc."[380]

"False zeal is against the sins of others, but he that has true zeal, exercises it chiefly against his own sins; though he shows also a proper zeal against prevailing and dangerous iniquity in others."[381]

3) Gracious affections are balanced and appropriate in their *steadfastness*.

"If therefore persons are religious only by fits and starts; if they now and then seem to be raised up to the clouds in their affections, and then suddenly fall down again, lose all, and become quite careless and carnal, and this is their manner of carrying on religion...they clearly evince their unsoundness."[382]

Jude 12-13
For example, Israel praised God for their deliverance at the Red Sea, but later longed to return to Egypt. Truly gracious affections, however, are of a more consistent and steadfast nature.

Jeremiah 17:7, 8
John 4:14

4) Gracious affections are balanced and appropriate in *public* and *private*.

"Some are greatly affected when in company, but have nothing that bears any manner of proportion to it in secret, in close meditation, secret prayer, and conversing with God, when alone and separated from all the world."[383]

"The Lord is neglected secretly, yet honoured openly; because there is no wind in their chambers to blow their sails; and therefore there they stand still. Hence many men keep their profession when they lose their affection. They have by the one a name to live (and that is enough) though their hearts be dead. And hence so long as you love and commend them, so long they love you; but if not, they will forsake you. They were warm only by another's fire, and hence, having no principle of life within, soon grow dead. This is the water that turns a Pharisee's mill."[384]

"The hypocrite (says Mr. Flavel) is not for the closet, but the synagogue, Matt. 6:5, 6. It is not his meat and drink to retire from the clamour of the world, to enjoy God in secret."[385]

---

[379] BT, 297; Yale, 370-371.
[380] BT, 297; Yale, 371.
[381] BT, 298; Yale, 317.
[382] BT, 298-299; Yale, 372.
[383] BT, 300; Yale, 374.
[384] Shepard, *Parable of the Ten Virgins*, 285; quoted in BT, 300, footnote; Yale, 374, footnote 4.
[385] Flavel, *Touchstone of Sincerity*. *Works* Vol. V, 567; quoted in BT, 300, footnote; Yale, 374, footnote 4.

Sign XI: The Higher Gracious Affections Are Raised, the Greater the Desire for Spiritual Growth, Whereas False Affections Rest Satisfied in Themselves

"The spiritual appetite after holiness and an increase of holy affections, is much more lively and keen in those that are eminent in holiness, than in others; and more when grace and holy affections are in their most lively exercise....The greatest eminence that the saints arrive at in this world has no tendency to satiety, or to abate their desires after more; but, on the contrary, makes them more eager to press forward."[386]

A) Support

    1 Corinthians 13:10-11
    2 Corinthians 1:22
    2 Corinthians 5:5
    Ephesians 1:14
    Philippians 3:13-15
    1 Peter 2:2-3

B) Why gracious affections increase the spiritual appetite for God

    1) The more grace believers have, the more they perceive God's holiness and how far they fall short.

    "The more persons have of holy affections, the more they have of that spiritual taste...whereby they perceive the excellency, and relish the divine sweetness, of holiness. And...the more they see their imperfection and emptiness, and distance from what ought to be: and so the more do they see their need of grace."[387]

    2) The nature of the imperfect recipient of grace desires to grow.

    "The greater spiritual discoveries and affections that a true Christian has, the more does he become an earnest beggar for grace and spiritual food, that he may grow."[388]

    Mark 9:24: "I do believe; help my unbelief."

C) A possible objection: Does not the Holy Spirit satisfy the soul?[389]

    Answer: Yes, relative to the things of the world, but not perfectly in this life.

    1) Relative to the things of the world

	The Spirit	The World
Satisfy the deepest needs of the soul?	Yes	No
Meet our expectation of satisfaction?	Yes	No
Satisfy permanently?	Yes	No
Are sufficient to satisfy to an infinite degree?	Yes	No

---

[386] BT, 303; Yale, 377.
[387] BT, 304; Yale 378.
[388] BT, 304; Yale, 378.
[389] BT, 304-305; Yale, 378-379.

2) But not perfectly in this life

> "If men be not satisfied here as to degree of happiness, the cause is with themselves; it is because they do not open their mouths wide enough."[390]

> "The more a man experiences and knows this excellent, unparalleled, exquisite, and satisfying sweetness, the more earnestly will he hunger and thirst for more, until he comes to perfection."[391]

D) The nature of false affections

1) False affections rest satisfied in their supposed religious attainments.

> "When false affections are raised very high, they put an end to longings after grace and holiness. The man now is far from appearing to himself a poor empty creature; on the contrary he is rich, and increased with goods, and hardly conceives of anything more excellent than what he has already attained to."[392]

In contrast to false affections:

> "Seeking God is spoken of as one of the distinguishing characters of the saints, and 'Seekers after God' is one of the names by which the godly are called in Scripture."[393]

Psalm 24:6
Psalm 69:6, 32
Psalm 70:4

2) False affections may be accompanied by an apparent seeking after God.

But:

> "Their desires [the hypocrites'] are not properly the desires of appetite after holiness for its own sake, or for the moral excellency and holy sweetness that is in it, but only for by-ends. They long after clearer discoveries that they may be better satisfied about the state of their souls; or because in great discoveries self is gratified, in being made so much of by God, and so exalted above others."[394]

Questions and Points for Discussion

1) We noted earlier that what may appear to be a love for God may merely be a love of the benefits of God. Is it also possible that seeking after God may merely be seeking after the benefits of God?

---

[390] BT, 305; Yale, 379.
[391] BT, 305; Yale, 379.
[392] BT, 306; Yale, 380.
[393] BT, 306; Yale, 381.
[394] BT, 307; Yale, 382.

2) Would Edwards view a commitment to others and the things of the church to the neglect of one's own wife and family as a fruit of the work of the Holy Spirit? Why or why not?

3) Review Edwards' categories of balance and symmetry noted above and identify areas in our culture or own personal lives that may exhibit a lack of proper balance. Does anyone get this perfectly right this side of glory?

4) Is it an evidence of the work of the Holy Spirit that someone is willing to serve people in poverty in the third world, forsaking their own personal comforts, but have no concern of the eternal destiny of those whom they serve? Why or why not?

5) Discuss the concept of the Holy Spirit satisfying our soul in Christ while yet our soul still craves more. Does contentment and satisfaction in Christ lead to carelessness and apathy? Why or why not?

Session Seventeen

Suggested Reading:

- *The Religious Affections*, Banner of Truth, 308-341; or
- *The Religious Affections*, Yale University Press, 383-420.

Sign XII: Gracious Affections Generate Christian Practice and Fruit (Part 1)

A) Implications

1) Gracious affections generate obedience to God's Word.[395]

    a) In abstaining from sin

    Matthew 5:29-30
    John 15:14
    1 John 3:3
    1 John 5:18

    b) In Christian service and charity

    Matthew 25:31-46

2) Gracious affections generate diligence and earnestness in the service of God.[396]

    Matthew 25:26, 30
    Philippians 3:13
    Titus 2:14
    Hebrews 6:11-12

3) Gracious affections generate perseverance in obedience and service to God.[397]

    a) Support

    Deuteronomy 32:18-20
    Jeremiah 17:13
    Ezekiel 3:20
    Matthew 10:22
    Matthew 13:4-8
    Matthew 24:13
    Luke 9:62
    John 8:30, 31
    John 15:6-16

---

[395] BT, 309-310; Yale, 384-387.
[396] BT, 310-312; Yale, 387-388.
[397] BT, 312-313; Yale, 388-389.

Romans 2:6-7
Romans 11:22
Colossians 1:22-23
Hebrews 3:6, 11-14
Hebrews 10:25-39
Revelation 2:11, 26

b) Qualification

"True saints may be guilty of some kinds and degrees of backsliding, may be foiled by particular temptations, and may fall into sin, yea great sins. But they never can fall away so as to grow weary of religion and the service of God, and habitually to dislike it and neglect it, either on its own account, or on account of the difficulties that attend it."[398]

Isaiah 43:22
Malachi 1:13
Romans 2:7
Galatians 6:9-10
Hebrews 10:36
James 4:4

B) Reasons why gracious affections generate Christian practice and fruit.

Because:

1) The source of gracious affections is God Himself, the Holy Spirit, exerting His nature in the exercises of the heart.

"The inward principal from whence they [gracious affections] flow is something divine, a communication of God, a participation of the divine nature, Christ living in the heart, the Holy Spirit dwelling there in union with the faculties of the soul, as an internal vital principle, exerting His own proper nature in the exercise of those faculties."[399]

"If God dwells in the heart, and is vitally united to it, He will show that He is a God, by the efficacy of His operation. Christ is not in the heart of a saint as in a sepulcher, or as a dead saviour that does nothing; but as in His temple, and as One that is alive from the dead. For in the heart where Christ savingly is, there He lives and exerts Himself after the power of that endless life that He received at His resurrection."[400]

Psalm 110:3
1 Corinthians 2:4
1 Corinthians 4:20
1 Thessalonians 1:5
2 Timothy 3:5

---

[398] BT, 313; Yale, 390.
[399] BT, 314-315; Yale, 392.
[400] BT, 315; Yale, 392.

2) The ground of gracious affections is the transcendently and lovable nature of God and His works, without reference to self-interest.[401]

> To summarize Edwards on this point, natural man pursues religion only so far as he perceives it to meet his self-interest, and no further. His involvement will change as his perceptions of the usefulness of religion to further his own self-interest changes. The saint's service, however, will not be so fluctuating, as the supreme motive for obedience and service is the infinite excellence of God who is eternally unchanging.

3) The ground of gracious affections is the moral excellency of God and His works.

> "That which men love, they desire to have and to be united to, and possessed of. That beauty which men delight in, they desire to be adorned with. Those acts which men delight in, they necessarily incline to do."[402]

> "By the sight of the transcendent glory of Christ, true Christians see Him worthy to be followed, and so are powerfully drawn after Him."[403]

4) Gracious affections are attended with the conviction that the Gospel is true.

> "They who were never thoroughly convinced that there is any reality in the things of religion, will never be at the labour and trouble of such an earnest, universal, and persevering practice of religion, through all difficulties, self-denials, and sufferings....On the other hand, they who are thoroughly convinced of the certain truth of those things must needs be governed by them in practice; for the things revealed in the Word of God are so great, and so infinitely more important than all other things."[404]

5) Gracious affections are attended with a change of nature.

> "Without a change of nature, men's practice will not be thoroughly changed. Until the tree be made good, the fruit will not be good. Men do not gather grapes of thorns, nor figs of thistles. The swine may be washed and appear clean for a little while but yet, without a change of nature, he will still wallow in the mire. Nature is a more powerful principle of action than anything that opposes it: though is may be violently restrained for a while, it will finally overcome that which restrains it."[405]

6) Gracious affections are attended with Christian humility.

> "A proud spirit is a rebellious spirit, but a humble spirit is a yieldable, subject, obediential spirit."[406]

7) Gracious affections are attended with a "lamb-like, dove-like spirit."

8) Gracious affections are attended with a tenderness of heart.

---

[401] BT, 316; Yale, 393-394.
[402] BT, 317; Yale, 394.
[403] BT, 317; Yale, 395.
[404] BT, 317-318; Yale, 395.
[405] BT, 318; Yale, 395.
[406] BT, 318-319; Yale, 396.

9) Gracious affections have a beautiful symmetry.

>Christian practice that is "universal, constant, and persevering" flows from gracious religious affections that are "universal and constant in all kinds of holy exercises, and towards all objects, and in all circumstances, and at all seasons, in a beautiful symmetry and proportion."[407]

10) Gracious affections produce a greater desire for God and spiritual things.

Thus, all the signs Edwards identifies as evidence of a true work of the Holy Spirit in a believer promote Christian practice.

C) Further support for the doctrine

1) "Having a heart to forsake all for Christ, tends to actually forsaking all for Him, so far as there is occasion, and we have trial. A having a heart to deny ourselves for Christ tends to a denying ourselves indeed, when Christ and self-interest stand in competition."[408]

2) True grace is active.

>"It is no barren thing; there is nothing in the universe that in its nature has a greater tendency to fruit. Godliness in the heart has as direct a relation to practice, as a fountain has to a stream, or as the luminous nature of the sun has to beams sent forth, or as life has to breathing."[409]

a) Christian practice is the nature and result of regeneration.

>"All is calculated and framed, in this mighty and manifold change wrought in the soul, so as directly to tend to this end."[410]

b) Christian practice is the purpose of Christ's redeeming work.

Ephesians 1:4
Ephesians 2:10
Titus 2:14

c) "Everything in a true Christian is calculated to reach this end."[411]

Matthew 3:10
Matthew 13:8, 23, 30-38
Matthew 21:19, 32-34
Luke 13:6
John 15:1-8
1 Corinthians 3:9
Hebrews 6:7-8

---

[407] BT, 319; Yale, 396.
[408] BT, 320; Yale, 397.
[409] BT, 320; Yale, 398.
[410] BT, 321; Yale, 398.
[411] BT, 321; Yale, 399.

3) True Christian practice is only found in true saints.

   a) The religion of the unregenerate is not enduring.

   "An unsanctified man may hide his sin, and may in many things, and for a season refrain from sin; but he will not be brought finally to renounce his sin, and give it a bill of divorce; sin is too dear to him, for him to be willing for that."[412]

   b) The religion of the unregenerate will not renounce self.

   "Herein chiefly consist the straightness of the gate, and the narrowness of the way that leads to life; upon the account of which, carnal men will not go in...that it is a way of utterly denying and finally renouncing all ungodliness, and so a way of self-denial or self-renunciation."[413]

   "Pharoah consented to let the people all go, and all that they had; but he was not steadfastly of that mind; he soon repented and pursued after them again, and the reason was, that those lusts of pride and covetousness that were gratified by Pharaoh's dominion over the people, and the gains of their service, were never really mortified in him, but only violently restrained."[414]

D) Christian practice and holy living display the sincerity of a Christian's profession.

1) The tree is known by its fruit.

   Matthew 5:16
   Matthew 7:16, 20
   Matthew 12:33
   Luke 6:44
   Philippians 2:21-22
   3 John 3-6

2) Actions speak louder than words.

   "Thus, if we see a man who in the course of his life seems to follow and imitate Christ, and greatly to exert and deny himself for the honour of Christ, and to promote His kingdom and interest in the world; reason teaches that this is an evidence of love to Christ, more to be depended on than if a man only says he has love to Christ, and tells of the inward experiences he has had of love to Him, what strong love he felt, and how his heart was drawn out in love at such and such a time, when it may be there appears but little imitation of Christ in his behaviour, and he seems backward to do any great matter for Him, or to put himself out of his way for the promoting of His kingdom."[415]

   "Passing affections easily produce words; and words are cheap; and godliness is more easily feigned in words than in actions. Christian practice is a costly, laborious thing. The self-denial that is required of Christians, and the narrowness of the way that leads to life, does not consist in words, but in practice."[416]

---

[412] BT, 324; Yale, 404.
[413] BT, 324; Yale, 404.
[414] BT, 326; Yale, 405.
[415] BT, 330-331; Yale, 330.
[416] BT, 332; Yale, 411.

John 14:21
James 2:18

<u>Note</u>: Edwards is not saying here that we should imitate the Pharisees and do good works from a desire to be seen and recognized by others. Rather, he is saying that the evidence of those transformed and indwelt by the Holy Spirit will be that they imitate Christ in their behavior.

E) Necessary qualifications to properly understand this doctrine.

1) A profession of the essentials of Christianity, implied or explicitly stated, is necessary, including (but not necessarily limited to):

   a) "We must profess that we believe that Jesus is the Messiah....that Jesus satisfied for our sins, and other essential doctrines of the gospel."[417]

   b) "It is essential to Christianity that we repent of our sins, that we be convinced of our own sinfulness, and that we are sensible we have justly exposed ourselves to God's wrath, and that our hearts do renounce all sin, and that we do with our whole hearts embrace Christ as our only Saviour; and that we love Him above all, and are willing for His sake to forsake all, and that we do give up ourselves to be entirely and forever His, etc."[418]

   c) "They should profess their faith in Jesus Christ, and that they embrace Christ, and rely upon Him as their Saviour with their whole hearts, and they do joyfully entertain the gospel of Christ."[419]

   d) "They should profess that they rely on Christ's righteousness only, and on His strength; and that they are devoted to Him, as their only Lord and Saviour, and that they rejoice in Him as their only righteousness and portion."[420]

2) The profession must be understood by the one making it

   a) The professing Christian must understand the meaning and personal implication of what they profess.

   A rote or superficial statement from "customary compliance" with established practice and form of testimony does not give evidence of a true profession of Christianity.[421]

   b) But, the distinct method and steps by which the Holy Spirit brought about conversion need not be understood.

   For a profession of Christianity to be considered acceptable, one need not understand the exact timing, steps, or method by which the Holy Spirit changed one's heart and brought one to faith. Some were insisting that one must be able to give an accurate account of such steps in order to be received into fellowship as a

---

[417] BT, 334; Yale, 413.
[418] BT, 334; Yale, 413.
[419] BT, 335; Yale, 414.
[420] BT, 335; Yale, 414.
[421] BT, 338; Yale, 417.

Christian, disregarding other evidences of true belief "that are vastly more important and essential."[422]

3) Christian practice is more than moral living and the absence of glaring character flaws. It involves a life devoted to the service and obedience to God.[423]

4) No external appearances are infallible evidences of grace.

"Nothing that appears to them in their neighbour can be sufficient to beget an absolute certainty concerning the state of his soul: for they see not his heart, nor can they see all his external behaviour. Much of it is in secret, and hid from the eye of the world; and it is impossible certainly to determine how far a man may go in many external appearances and imitations of grace, from other principles."[424]

Questions and Points for Discussion

1) Why do gracious affections produce obedience, diligence, and perseverance in Christian practice?

2) Can a true Christian stumble and fall away from faith in Christ? Why or why not?

3) How is the present sign of Christian practice related to the first distinguishing sign that gracious affections are the fruit of the Holy Spirit that dwells permanently in the believer?

---

[422] BT, 339; Yale, 418.
[423] BT, 339-340; Yale, 418-420.
[424] BT, 340-341; Yale, 420.

4) What is the most obvious criterion for determining that someone's religious affections are not gracious (produced by the Holy Spirit and evidence that the person is a believer)?

5) What distinguishes true Christian practice from non-Christian outward religious and moral practice?

6) What are some implications of Edwards' qualification that no external appearances are *infallible* evidences of grace, especially in light of the fact that he makes the statement in the midst of his giving evidences of grace?

SESSION EIGHTEEN

Suggested Reading:

- *The Religious Affections*, Banner of Truth, 341-364; or
- *The Religious Affections*, Yale University Press, 420-444.

Sign XII: Gracious Affections Generate Christian Practice and Fruit (Part 2)

F) Christian practice and assurance of salvation

1) Christian practice is sure evidence to our conscience that we are a sincere Christian.

   a) Support:

   Psalm 119:6
   Matthew 7:16-24
   Galatians 6:4
   Hebrews 6:9ff.
   1 John 2:3
   1 John 3:18-19

   b) The inclination of the heart (will) producing action is the primary evidence of grace to the conscience.

   "As God looks at the obedience and practice of the man, He looks at the practice of the soul; for the soul is the man in God's sight, 'for the Lord seeth not as man seeth, for he looketh on the heart.'"[425]

   "When practice is given as a sure evidence of our real Christianity to our own consciences, then is meant *that* in our practice which is visible to our own consciences; which is not only the motion of our bodies, but the exertion of the soul, which directs and commands that motion; which is more directly and immediately under the view of our own consciences, than the acts of the body."[426]

   "What is inward is of greatest importance, yet what is outward is included and intended, as connected with the practical exertion of grace in the will, directing and commanding the actions of the body."[427]

   Isaiah 38:3
   Jeremiah 17:10
   John 13:34-35
   John 14:21
   John 15:10-14
   1 John 2:3, 7-11
   Revelation 2:23

---

[425] BT, 344-345; Yale, 424.
[426] BT, 345; Yale, 424.
[427] BT, 346; Yale, 425.

2) Christian practice, including the disposition of the heart generating it, is the *chief evidence* to one's conscience of the sincerity of one's faith in Christ.

   a) Support: Six arguments

      i) A man's practice reveals the preference of his heart.

> "The main and most proper proof of his having an heart to anything, concerning which he is at liberty to follow his own inclinations, and either to do or not to do as he pleases, is his doing of it. When a man is at liberty whether to speak or keep silence, the most proper evidence of his having a heart to speak, is his speaking. When a man is at liberty whether to walk or sit still, the proper proof of his having a heart to walk, is his walking. Godliness consists not in a heart which intends to do the will of God, but in a heart which does it."[428]

Deuteronomy 5:27-29

      ii) Trials reveal the true heart.

> "Holy practice, under trials, is the highest evidence of the sincerity of professors to their own consciences."[429]

> "For when God is said by these things to try men and prove them, to see what is in their hearts and whether they will keep His commandments or no, we are not to understand, that it is for His own information, or that He may obtain evidence Himself of their sincerity (for He needs no trials for His information); but chiefly for their conviction and to exhibit evidence to their consciences."[430]

> "Seeing therefore that these are the things that God makes use of to try us, it is undoubtedly the surest way for us to pass a right judgment on ourselves, to try ourselves by the same things....The surest way to know our gold is to look upon it and examine it in God's furnace, where He tries it for that end, that we may see what it is. If we have a mind to know whether a building stands strong or no, we must look upon it when the wind blows. If we would know whether that which appears in the form of wheat, has real substance of wheat, or is only chaff, we must observe it when it is winnowed. If we would know whether a staff is strong, or a rotten broken reed, we must observe it when it is leaned on and weight is borne upon it. If we would weigh ourselves justly, we must weigh ourselves in the scales that God makes use of to weigh us."[431]

      iii) Grace is said to be made perfect or finished in Christian practice.

> "The tree is made perfect in the fruit; it is not perfected in the seed's being planted in the ground; it is not perfected in the first quickening of the seed, and in its putting forth root and sprout; nor is it perfected when it comes up out of the ground; nor is it perfected in bringing forth leaves; nor yet in putting forth blossoms: but when it has brought forth good ripe fruit, then it is perfected,

---

[428] BT, 348; Yale, 427.
[429] BT, 352-353; Yale, 432.
[430] BT, 352; Yale, 431.
[431] BT, 353; Yale, 432-433.

therein it reaches its end, the design of the tree is finished: all that belongs to the tree is completed and brought to its proper effect in the fruit."[432]

"If we would see the proper nature of anything whatsoever, and see it in its full distinction from other things, let us look upon it in the finishing of it."[433]

James 2:22
1 John 2:4-5
1 John 4:12, 17, 18-19

iv) Holy practice as evidence of the sincerity and reality of one's Christian profession is the principal of all other evidences noted in Scripture.

"This [holy practice] is ten times more insisted on as a note of true piety throughout the Scripture, from the beginning of Genesis to the end of Revelation, than anything else."[434]

"There is no one virtuous affection or disposition so often expressly spoken of as a sign of true grace, as our having love one to another: but then the Scriptures explain themselves to intend chiefly this love as exercised and expressed in practice, or in deeds of love."[435]

Matthew 22:39-40
Romans 8:7-10
Galatians 5:14
1 John 3:14

A Needed Caution: "To insist much on those things that the Scripture insists little on, and to insist very little on those things on which the Scripture insists much, is a dangerous thing; because it is going out of God's way, and is to judge ourselves in an unscriptural manner. God knew which way of leading and guiding souls was safest and best for them: He insisted so much on some things, because He knew it to be needful that they should be insisted on; and let other things more alone as a wise God, because He knew it was not best for us so much to lay the weight of the trial there....And for us to make that great which the Scripture makes little, and that little which the Scripture makes great, tends to give us a monstrous idea of religion; and (at least indirectly and gradually) to lead us wholly away from the right rule, and from a right opinion of ourselves, and to establish delusion and hypocrisy."[436]

v) Christian practice is presented in Scripture as the main evidence of true grace to our own conscience.

Psalm 15:1-2
Psalm 24:3-4
Psalm 119:1, 6
Proverbs 8:13

---

[432] BT, 355; Yale, 435.
[433] BT, 356; Yale, 436.
[434] BT, 356; Yale, 436.
[435] BT, 357; Yale, 437.
[436] BT, 358; Yale, 438.

John 8:31
John 14:15, 21, 23-24
John 15:2, 8, 14
1 Corinthians 6:9-10
Galatians 6:7-8
Ephesians 5:5-6
James 1:26-27
1 John 1:6
1 John 2:3-5
1 John 3:6-10, 18-19
1 John 5:3
2 John 6

vi) People will be judged according to their works at the judgment seat of God, revealing the righteousness of God's righteous judgment to the conscience of those professing belief and to the world.

"For God's future judging of men in order to their eternal retribution, will not be His trying, and finding out, and passing a judgment upon the state of men's hearts, in His own mind; but it will be a declarative judgment; and the end of it will be not God's forming a judgment within Himself, but the manifestation of His judgment and the righteousness of it to men's own consciences, and to the world."[437]

Jeremiah 17:10
Jeremiah 32:19
Proverbs 24:12
Matthew 25:31-46
Romans 2:5-13
1 Corinthians 5:10
1 Peter 1:17
Revelation 2:23
Revelation 20:12-13
Revelation 22:12

3) Summary of the relationship of Christian practice to assurance

"Now from all that has been said, I think it to be abundantly manifest that Christian practice is the most proper evidence of the gracious sincerity of professors, to themselves and others; and the chief of all the marks of grace, the sign of signs, and evidence of evidences, that which seals and crowns all other signs."[438]

"There may be several good evidences that a tree is a fig-tree; but the highest and most proper evidence of it is that it actually bears figs."[439]

---

[437] BT, 361; Yale, 441.
[438] BT, 363; Yale, 443.
[439] BT, 363; Yale, 443.

Questions and Points for Discussion

1) In introducing the twelve distinguishing signs, Edwards noted that "assurance is not to be obtained so much by *self-examination* as by *action*."[440] How does this statement relate to Christian practice as evidence of our salvation?

2) We are not saved by works, but God will judge us by our works, why?

3) Why is Christian practice the *chief evidence* to one's conscience of the sincerity of one's faith in Christ?

4) Many who professed faith in Christ and were zealous for Christian practice during the Awakening later fell into sinful lifestyles and became disinterested in the things of Christ. Yet, they still claimed to be saved based on their past experience. According to Edwards, what does this evidence tell you of the nature of their spiritual experience and state before God?

5) Some of these same people who fell into disinterest and sinful lifestyles became worried about their lack of assurance of salvation. How does their situation relate to Edwards' arguments concerning Christian practice as evidence to one's own conscience? Would Edwards council them to not doubt their salvation? Why or why not?

---

[440] BT, 123; Yale, 195.

Session Nineteen

Suggested Reading:

- *The Religious Affections*, Banner of Truth, 364-375; or
- *The Religious Affections*, Yale University Press, 444-455.

Sign XII: Gracious Affections Generate Christian Practice and Fruit (Part 3)

G) Christian practice "is the great evidence which confirms and crowns all other signs of godliness."[441] Holy practice is stated in Scripture to be the proper evidence of the following:[442]

1) True and saving knowledge of God

    1 John 1:6
    1 John 2:3

2) Repentance

    Matthew 3:8
    Acts 26:20

3) Saving faith

    James 2:21-24

4) Belief of the truth

    3 John 3

5) True faith in Christ so as to forsake all for Him

    "To forsake all for Christ in heart is the same thing as to have a heart actually to forsake all; but the proper evidence of having a heart actually to forsake all, is, indeed, actually to forsake all so far as called to it."[443]

    Luke 5:27, 28

6) Trust in Christ for salvation

    Matthew 10:39
    2 Timothy 1:12
    Hebrews 11:24

---

[441] BT, 364; Yale, 444.
[442] BT, 364-370; Yale, 444-449.
[443] BT, 366; Yale, 446.

7) Love to God and man

8) Humility

9) The true fear of God

> Job 1:8
> Psalm 34:11
> Psalm 36:1
> Proverbs 3:7
> Proverbs 8:13

10) True thankfulness

> Psalm 116:12

11) A gracious hope

> 1 Thessalonians 1:2-3
> 1 Peter 1:13-14
> 1 John 3:3

12) A truly holy joy

> Psalm 119:111-112
> 1 Corinthians 13:6

13) Christian fortitude

> 1 Corinthians 9:25-27
> 2 Timothy 2:3-5

H) Two possible objections to the doctrine that Christian practice is the chief of all signs of saving grace

1) <u>Objection One</u>: The above doctrine appears contrary to what has already been said, that the greatest evidence of God's saving work in a believer involves the inward experience of the heart.[444]

<u>But</u>:

a) Holy practice cannot be separated and distinguished from the experience of the heart.

"Holy practice is the holy action of the mind, directing and governing the motions of the body. And the motions of the body are to be looked upon as belonging to Christian practice, only secondarily, and as they are dependent and consequent on the acts of the soul."[445] In other words, outward actions are dependent upon the inward heart (will).

---

[444] BT, 370-375; Yale, 450-455.
[445] BT, 371; Yale, 450.

"To speak of Christian experience and practice as if they were two things properly and entirely distinct, is to make a distinction without consideration or reason. Indeed, all Christian experience is not properly called practice, but all Christian practice is properly experience."[446]

"These inward exercises are not the less a part of Christian experience because they have outward behaviour immediately connected with them."[447]

b) Though Christianity is supremely a relationship of the heart between God and man, holy practice is the most important and distinguishing part of this inward spiritual experience.

Jeremiah 22:15-16
Romans 1:9
2 Corinthians 1:12
2 Corinthians 4:13
2 Corinthians 5:7, 14
2 Corinthians 6:4-7
Galatians 2:20
Colossians 1:29
1 Thessalonians 2:2, 8-10
2 Timothy 4:6-7
1 John 5:3
2 John 6

c) True Christian practice, therefore, is most properly called experimental religion [religion of experience or of the heart].

"There is a sort of external religious practice, without inward experience, which in the sight of God is esteemed good for nothing. And there is what is called experience, that is without practice, being neither accompanied nor followed with a Christian behaviour; and this is worse than nothing."[448]

"Religion consists much in holy affections; but those exercises of affection which are most distinguishing of true religion are these practical exercises. Friendship between earthly friends consists much in affection; but those strong exercises of affection that actually carry them through fire and water for each other are the highest evidences of true friendship."[449]

d) The witness of the Holy Spirit that we are sons of God is often most conspicuous in our obedience under severe trials.

"The witness or seal of the Spirit that we read of doubtless consists in the effect of the Spirit of God on the heart, in the implantation and exercises of grace there, and so consists in experience. And it is also beyond doubt, that this seal of the Spirit is the highest kind of evidence of the saints' adoption that ever they obtain."[450]

---

[446] BT, 371; Yale, 450-451.
[447] BT, 371; Yale, 450.
[448] BT, 373; Yale, 452.
[449] BT, 373-374; Yale, 453.
[450] BT, 374; Yale, 454.

"It has been abundantly found to be true in fact, by the experience of the Christian church, that Christ commonly gives, by His Spirit, the greatest and most joyful evidences to His saints of their sonship in those effectual exercises of grace under trials...as is manifest in the full assurance and unspeakable joys of many of the martyrs."[451]

Romans 5:2-3
Romans 8:15-18
2 Corinthians 5:5
1 Peter 4:14
Revelation 2:13, 17

Questions and Points for Discussion

1) What is the relationship of faith, repentance, and love to Christian practice?

2) Do Christ's words in John 14:12-21 support Edwards' arguments? If so, how?

3) Explain what Edwards means by "all Christian experience is not properly called practice, but all Christian practice is properly experience."[452]

4) According to Edwards, why can two people perform identical outward acts, though the acts of one are condemned by God and the other's same acts are rewarded by God?

5) Discuss how and why one's actions and attitude in the midst of persecution are an evidence of a true work of God in a believer.

---

[451] BT, 374-375; Yale, 454.
[452] BT, 371; Yale, 450-451.

Session Twenty

Suggested Reading:

- *The Religious Affections*, Banner of Truth, 375-382; or
- *The Religious Affections*, Yale University Press, 455-461.

Sign XII: Gracious Affections Generate Christian Practice and Fruit (Part 4)

2) <u>Objection Two</u>: Christian practice as the chief evidence of true grace in the heart is legalistic and inconsistent with justification by faith alone.

   But:

   a) Christian practice follows the gift of salvation as a result of the gift, but in no way precedes the free gift or is a cause of it.

   "But this objection is altogether without reason....It is our works being the price of God's favour, and not their being the sign of it, that is the thing which is inconsistent with the freeness of that favour. Surely the beggar's looking on the money he has in his hands, as a sign of the kindness of him who gave it to him, is in no respect inconsistent with the freeness of that kindness."[453]

   "And this is the notion of justification without works (as this doctrine is taught in the Scripture), that it is not the worthiness or loveliness of our works, or anything in us, which is in anywise accepted with God, as a balance for the guilt of sin, or a recommendation of sinners to His acceptance as heirs of life. Thus we are justified only by the righteousness of Christ, and not by our righteousness."[454]

   <u>Note</u>: New life in Christ necessarily produces a changed life, but to assert a necessary result of salvation must therefore be a cause of salvation is illogical and unbiblical. Christian works follow salvation but can never merit salvation, for Christ alone satisfied the sinless perfection and penalty required by God's justice for the salvation of sinners. Justification, therefore, can only be by the imputation of Christ's perfect righteousness to the one united to Christ by faith.[455]

   b) If Christian practice as evidence of God's grace is inconsistent with salvation by free grace, then all other evidence of God's grace in the heart are inconsistent with salvation by free grace, such as love of God, joy, self-emptiness, etc.

   Under the objector's logic, there can be nothing as evidence of the grace of God in one's life, apart from a profession of belief. This, however, is contrary to the overwhelming weight of what Scripture presents as evidence of God's grace in a believer's life.

---

[453] BT, 376; Yale, 455.
[454] BT, 376; Yale, 455.
[455] For an in-depth exposition of Edwards' understanding of the merit of Christ's righteousness as the sole basis of salvation, see Biehl, *The Infinite Merit of Christ*.

c) Scripture does not present the absolute necessity of holy practice to be inconsistent with free grace.

Proverbs 9:4-6
Isaiah 1:16ff.
Isaiah 55:1-3, 7
Revelation 3:20-21
Revelation 21:6, 7
Revelation 22:14-15

"So that if any are against such an importance of holy practice as has been spoken of, it must be only from a senseless aversion to the letters and sound of the word *works*, when there is no reason in the world to be given for it, but what may be given with equal force, why they should have an aversion to the words *holiness, godliness, grace, religion, experience,* and even *faith* itself; for to make a righteousness of any of these is as legal, and as inconsistent with the way of the new covenant, as to make a righteousness of holy practice."[456]

d) It is both dangerous and wrong to de-emphasize or second-guess that which God has revealed in His Word.

"It is greatly to the hurt of religion for persons to make light of, and insist little on, those things which the Scripture insists most upon as of most importance in the evidence of our interest in Christ, under a notion that to lay weight on these things is legal"[457]

"It is our wisdom not to take His work out of His hands, but to follow Him, and lay the stress of the judgment of ourselves there where He has directed us. If we do otherwise, no wonder if we are bewildered, confounded, and fatally deluded. But if we had got into the way of looking chiefly at those things which Christ and His apostles and prophets chiefly insisted on, and so in judging of ourselves and others, chiefly regarding practical exercises and effects of grace, not neglecting other things, it would be of manifold happy consequence. It would above all things tend to the conviction of deluded hypocrites, and to prevent the delusion of those whose hearts were never brought to a thorough compliance with the straight and narrow way which leads to life."[458]

"It would become fashionable for men to show their Christianity, more by an amiable distinguished behaviour, than by an abundant and excessive declaring their experiences....A great many of the main stumbling blocks against experimental and powerful religion would be removed, and religion would be declared and manifested in such a way that, instead of hardening spectators, and exceedingly promoting infidelity and atheism, it would, above all things, tend to convince men that there is a reality in religion....Thus the light of professors would so shine before men, that others, seeing their good works, would glorify their Father which is in heaven."[459]

---

[456] BT, 380; Yale, 459.
[457] BT, 380; Yale, 459.
[458] BT, 381; Yale, 460-461.
[459] BT, 382; Yale, 461.

Questions and Points for Discussion

1) Discuss Edwards' assertion that Christian practice is not the cause of salvation, but is the necessary result of salvation. Why is this not justification by works?

2) Smoke always follows fire, but smoke does not cause fire. Give other examples of things that necessarily follow something but are not its cause.

3) Edwards contends that if holy practice, as the necessary fruit or effect of salvation, is inconsistent with salvation by grace, then all of the inward graces of the Holy Spirit as the necessary fruit and effect of salvation are also inconsistent with salvation by grace. Why?

4) How does the first distinguishing sign relate to the eleven other distinguishing signs?

5) According to Edwards, why is it important to understand the difference between the twelve uncertain signs and the twelve distinguishing signs?

6) Will the twelve distinguishing signs always be visible to others?

7) How is *The Religious Affections* applicable to the church today? How is it applicable to our own personal life in Christ?

www.ingramcontent.com/pod-product-compliance
Lightning Source LLC
Chambersburg PA
CBHW080443110426
42743CB00016B/3255